ANOMALY

ANOMALY

How to Finally
STAND OUT
from the Crowd

ZACK MILLER

NEW YORK

LONDON • NASHVILLE • MELBOURNE • VANCOUVER

ANOMALY
How to Finally STAND OUT *from the Crowd*

© 2019 **ZACK MILLER**

Published in New York, New York, by Morgan James Publishing. Morgan James is a trademark of Morgan James, LLC. www.MorganJamesPublishing.com

The Morgan James Speakers Group can bring authors to your live event. For more information or to book an event visit The Morgan James Speakers Group at www.TheMorganJamesSpeakersGroup.com.

ISBN 978-1-64279-175-4 paperback
ISBN 978-1-64279-176-1 eBook
ISBN 978-1-64279-180-8 hardcover
Library of Congress Control Number: 2018907830

Cover Design and Interior Graphics by:
Dave Ritt

Interior Design by:
Bonnie Bushman
The Whole Caboodle Graphic Design

In an effort to support local communities, raise awareness and funds, Morgan James Publishing donates a percentage of all book sales for the life of each book to Habitat for Humanity Peninsula and Greater Williamsburg.

Get involved today! Visit
www.MorganJamesBuilds.com

ACKNOWLEDGEMENTS

To my amazing wife, Meghan. Thank you for always being my rock. And to Ashebrooke, the best friend a man could ever wish for.

To Dave Ritt, Tim Ryan, Chelsea Nettleton, Chris Hill, Brittany and David Peregoff, Luvenia Hankins, Chris Jones, Scott McJunkin, and, of course, Morgan James Publishing for playing a pivotal role in making *Anomaly* stronger.

To those of you who believed in *Anomaly* in its early stages. Thank you. To Chad Stenzel, Jim Carroll, Jessica Bertsch, Dusty Williams, Joyce, Kevin Hughes, Shane Richardson, Jim Hurley, Glen Glover, Mindy L. Hughes, APR, Matthew Diggs, John Fuller, Cory Blackburn, Jeraud Norman, Kassie Simpson, Mark Rowan, George Berry—BFF, Heather MF Herrick, Christopher G. Shelton, Chuck Williams, Gary Plaag, Nancy Grden, David Sullivan, Brian Baublitz, Erica McMannes, Richard Chaing suffolkexecutiveoffices.com, Anchorage Barbershop, Heather Myers, Ben "The Pun Master" Wallace, Joe Fuller, Tracy Link, Jeremy Johnson, Martin Joseph, Tim Masterson, Scott Janney, Rick Miller, Tiffanie Rosier, T.J. Reid, Xerxes Nabong, Cassidy Lewis, Sonya Schweitzer, Larry Lombardi, Sharon Miller, Sonya Phillips, and J Donnelly.

TABLE OF CONTENTS

INTRODUCTION

I went from being miserable out of college and meeting people on the worst day of their lives to someone who followed a different path, the path not often talked about. The path of creating one's own life. I'm married now, incredibly happy, and have created a business career many would die for. I've won dozens of awards and met and interviewed thousands of people, including Daymond John of *Shark Tank*, who is the founder of the billion-dollar company FUBU. I've talked business at the White House, hosted a TV show on ABC, signed with Morgan James Publishing to release *Anomaly*, and I've helped a lot of people along the way. Most importantly, I'm happy. I am happy I didn't get stuck where so many are—in a black hole that seems impossible to crawl out of.

Back in 2010, I was sick of working for the man, so I quit. After 1,095 days working for a CBS television station in Norfolk, VA, I'd had enough. I was miserable. After work, I'd head to the local watering hole to have a few too many.

You don't realize how terrible your situation is until you get out and reflect. I knew that I wasn't happy. I made a measly $25,000 a year. Colleagues at other TV stations respected me, but not the colleagues and superiors at my own station.

I followed the path I was taught to walk—not by my parents, but by society. The path that urges you to get good grades in order to get into a top-notch college so that you can then get a job working your way up the corporate ladder.

Just writing that makes me want to puke, which is ironic because I was good at my craft—a journalist—which consisted of covering the news stories of the day, weather, and breaking news. I was one of the local celebrities, recognizable at the local watering hole and even walking down the street. Anyone would be envious of my position but meeting someone on the worst day of their life day after day became an emotional strain on me. I couldn't handle interviewing one more elderly lady grieving the loss of her grandson to senseless gang violence. I couldn't handle the bickering of politics, the overseas wars, and the ubiquitous bad news filling nearly every minute of the news hour. Those stories had become my reality, and my reality was in dire need of a change.

I questioned my life choices at this point. How did I end up here? I felt stuck. What else could I do with a journalism degree? *Why* did I get a journalism degree? I felt like I couldn't just quit. That would be a waste of the last five years of my life and tens of thousands of dollars in student loans. I wanted more out of my career, but it didn't matter if I moved to a different city or to a different TV station. It was the same job with a different location. It was the same job over and over. It was the same stories every single day. I was better than this monotony, and to make matters worse, I got into a bit of trouble at work. Instead of being suspended, or worse, fired, I had to check in with my director every day to talk about what I worked on the day before and what I would be working on that day. Talk about babysitting and being treated like I was incompetent. This predicament didn't help the second-guessing of my career.

Don't get me wrong. Through all of this there were positives, and to the naked eye, you may never have thought Zack was going through a tough time. I won awards, was in good shape, I lived on the beach, was fresh out of college, and was mostly single. But I hated going to work every day and I wanted to change it.

I spent a year trying to find which types of jobs I could do with my skills. The same job kept coming up on job boards to do same thing I was doing in TV, just housed at a different place. But, now that I left my job as a journalist—the one I spent five years at West Virginia University and cashed out $80,000 in student loans preparing for—I didn't know what to do. So, I jumped off the cliff and needed to survive. I was a nobody, literally. I was getting into a world where I had zero relationships. I needed to quickly create some since my life now depended on it.

Two things happened.

1. I looked through the relationships I already had and saw where they overlapped from my journalism world and now into the business world. Taking an inventory of your life can be done by looking through yearbooks, online accounts, emails, directories, and/or anywhere you have a relationship. There was a colleague of mine from TV news whose family owned a small public relations business, Rubin Communications Group in Virginia Beach, VA. I reached out and introduced myself. A decade later, that relationship is still strong.

2. I read *Get Clients Now!* by C.J. Hayden. She says if you're a nobody in life or in business that is okay because everyone has to start somewhere. But what do you do? You invite those who you want a relationship with to your office through small educational events.

In college, I threw parties several weekends a year. Nobody wants to go to a party that sucks. If your party sucks, the guests you want won't show up or bail once they arrive and notice how lackluster it is. To get guests to my events (or parties during college), I picked up the phone and invited them (or texted or emailed). The key is you *must* invite individuals and not just post an event on Facebook (or a flyer on a college board) if you expect people to attend. It sounds simple, but that individual attention will increase your probability of getting guests.

Over the past decade, I went from a successful award-winning journalist to a successful award-winning businessman. I didn't go to business school. I didn't get an MBA. I didn't have a lot of money (or any money). But, I did have effort, hustle, and the willingness to learn and execute. All of the keys to success I learned over the past decade will be detailed in the following pages. Tips and tricks that have been tested over and over with different people and different scenarios. Techniques that will show you ways over, around, or through your obstacles.

An anomaly is defined as something that deviates from what's standard, normal, or expected. So, as a new "businessman" I had to be different. I had to be the anomaly. I'll show you how I used being an anomaly to turn myself into a well-respected, successful businessman. One who can land any meeting by following the methods and techniques in this book.

I wrote this as a blueprint, including step-by-step instructions on how to become the anomaly. I understand that most people reading this book aren't already millionaires, so the methods and techniques you'll learn about are either free to implement or super cheap. This book was written so you can go back to specific chapters when you have questions. If you get stuck on a concept, go back to that chapter for clarity. At the end of every chapter, you'll find a roadmap which encompasses a series of next steps for you to take referring back to the chapter you just read. You can download the Anomaly Method Roadmap (AMR) and all of its assets and resources at AnomalyMethod.com.

Disclaimer: You have to test what will work for you and your business. No two situations are alike. So, just because a specific approach worked for Jane, you might have to make some minor adjustments to make it work for you. Go into this book with an experimental mindset. Have fun with it. Tweak this and that until you figure out what works for you.

PART 1

THE SALES FUNNEL

1	Free Content
2	Mutual Data Point
3	Supplemental Info
4	Dig Deep
5	Hard Sell
6	24-Hr Follow-Up
7	Post Sale

Chapter 1

WHY WHAT YOU'RE DOING ISN'T WORKING

Everyone in the world was born to be something, yet society pushes us all to play by a specific set of rules. Primarily, do good in school so that you can get into college. Then pick a major at college that will help you get a job upon graduation. Then work at a company for the rest of your life while moving up the corporate ladder. It sounds lovely until you realize that you might not be "school smart" and wouldn't be able to get into a great college. Or, if you did go to college, maybe you chose the wrong major. Then when you graduated college and got a corporate job, you realized that you chose wrong. You hate the industry and are miserable. You want more with the career or business that you're in. It doesn't matter if you own the business or are a teammate, we all have skills and to get the most out of them you must use them, in a vehicle that allows you to succeed.

Being an anomaly is about doing something different than others. It can be physical, as in the way you move or dress or from a process standpoint. It can also be the way you speak or respond. Don't be afraid to start something. Stop waiting for the perfect timing because you'll be waiting the rest of your life. You have to start somewhere, so don't let lack of confidence be your reason for not starting. You'll get better along the way. You don't have to be the best, but you can do it differently. Being an anomaly is standing out or being noticed. Throughout this book, you'll learn techniques and strategies as well as guides and templates to make this happen for you.

Whether you're a business owner, a college graduate looking for a job, or are just unhappy in your current position, *Anomaly* provides the business principles to get the results or conversions you desire. **Conversions are the successful events where your target customer completes the action you're trying to get them to do.** Examples of conversions range from buying a product from your store, signing a contract, getting a girl to go out with you, or subscribing to your email list.

Throughout *Anomaly* are words like brand, personality, personal brand, or business. These words are used in business as ways of describing you and/or your business. By creating or improving one of these areas, you'll see results that will accelerate faster than a rocket into space.

A target customer is the person or group of people that you have identified to have a series of similar trends and are interested in the products or services you provide. For example, this target customer could be the boss or hiring manager at the company where you desire to work. The sale to your target customer could look like a number of different things—the typical sale of a product or service, the sale of yourself in an interview situation, or getting someone to subscribe to your content. Every business has a target customer and it's important to know who that customer is and what that customer looks like. Details about your target customer influence almost every decision made in your business: logo design, marketing channels, email copy, photography choices, etc.

Are you a fan of salesy people who want you for your money? Most likely not. So, why would you want to make your target customers feel that way? Instead, create a lasting relationship with the target customer before trying to sell them anything. To make an even stronger case about target customers, instead of thinking of them as targets or prospects, first think of them as potential friends. Start with a desire to create a lasting friendship. People often won't support or buy from people they don't know, but they love to support people they like, trust, and have a relationship with. If you can take that deeper and have a true friendship with them, you improve your chances of a conversion. What's worse than being sold to is when you're being sold something that you don't want. Your local cable company likely comes to mind. Instead of creating similar procedures to them, create one-to-one relationships and you'll see your results flourish.

Value is providing something useful to someone. If you're an accountant, you help someone with their taxes. If you're a comedian, the value you provide is making someone laugh. What are you best at and who is looking for it? When you're unknown and trying to be seen, you have to do things to get noticed, such as throwing events that normally would be hosted by a Chamber of Commerce, Facebook Live videos on topics no one is talking about, even dressing differently, dying your hair, driving a weird car, or bringing your dog to work. These are nonstandard things in the world and could make people do a double take. Once you have their attention, it's time to provide value.

The concept of marketing is simple. Marketing is doing anything to get someone's attention or get them to look at you or your business. If they never see you, they'll never see your message, product, service, etc. Once they see you, if their first interaction or experience is positive, there's a much higher likelihood they'll take the next step with you. Studies show that it takes about six occurrences to be noticed. That is potentially six interactions with you and/or your marketing before your message will get across and sink in enough for them to take the next steps.

Think about when you're scrolling through your newsfeed on social media. What do you stop for? Cute puppies and kittens? Maybe. Fainting goats? Probably. Ads? Most likely no unless they're intensely clever or funny. So, how do you get someone to stop scrolling when they see your ad? You have to be different. When you attend a networking event, the overwhelming majority of the audience looks the same. What can you do to stand out? I go to a lot of networking events. Usually the room is filled with suits and everyone looks the same. To set myself apart, I wear jeans, a black T-shirt, and sneakers. When you stick out, people want to see what you're all about. What makes this person so different?

What can you do with your business cards or website to set yourself apart? Do you own a dog-walking service? What if you did paw-shaped business cards instead of the traditional rectangular ones? Think outside the marketing box.

Look at Chick-fil-A. Many of their billboards are three-dimensional, which immediately catches your attention, unlike boring text and/or image-only billboards. Or how about on television? Some companies add a period of silence

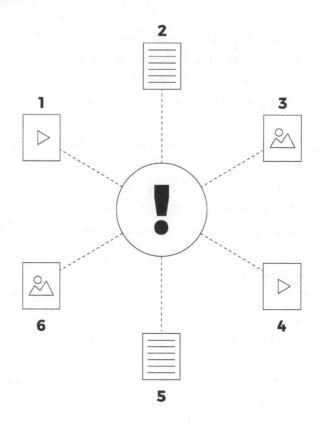

6 Occurrences to Be Noticed

in their ads to get people's attention. If you want to be an anomaly, explore every possibility and don't be afraid to be different.

Now, advertising is expensive, and Chick-fil-A is a mega-brand, but you can still learn from their tactics and implement their strategies. Dissect what a big brand is doing at the core to get attention and figure out ways to do it within your budget. *When it comes to marketing, money isn't the vehicle that engages a person's eyeballs—it's setting yourself apart from the pack.*

Do you remember learning about compound interest in economics class back in high school or college? The earlier you start saving, the more you save because interest compounds. Creating an audience follows the same rule, especially online. The sooner you create your channels and offer valuable content, the sooner you'll attract your target customer. The sooner you attract your target customer, the sooner you can develop a relationship with them. And the sooner you develop a relationship, the sooner you can convert them to a client and not just a friend. That is the ultimate goal of marketing.

-------------- **Roadmap** --------------

1. Download the Anomaly Method Roadmap (AMR) at AnomalyMethod.com.
2. Decide on your goal or conversion to track.

Chapter 2

THE FUNDAMENTALS NO ONE TAUGHT YOU

I f you're reading this book, you might be an entrepreneur. Even if you're not, I think we'd both agree that embracing the entrepreneurial mindset is critical in today's business world. It can be difficult to keep from thinking on a grand scale (i.e., How can I become the next Amazon or Facebook?). But, do you have unlimited time and money? Are you a company with over a decade under your belt? When thinking about big brands and how you might become one, you can't look at where those companies are today. You need to think about where they started.

All mega-brands started small. Amazon was an online bookstore, and Facebook was a college directory for students at a college in Boston. These two companies were trying to solve a problem. To become an anomaly, you need to find the "problem" that you're trying to solve, also known as your niche. **A niche is a subset of the market that involves a specialized industry or area.** The market is small, but so is the competition. A good example of a niche is someone specializing in refurbishing vintage stereos.

In the late 1990s, the Internet wasn't a trusted entity. It wasn't part of everyday life like it is today. However, Jeff Bezos knew what could come of it. He started small but kept his vision wide. One of the most important things you need to do is maintain vision and focus. Keep an eye on your long-term plan but focus and work hard on what's in front of you.

Your focus should be to provide lasting value to your customer's everyday life. This may come as a surprise, but your prospect doesn't wake up thinking about you. However, as you become an everyday occurrence, you can move the needle little by little to integrate your brand into their lives. Similar to how adoring fans anxiously await a new season of *Lost* or *Stranger Things,* people want more of what they love. So, make them love you. It's possible to provide so much value, content, help, and support that they can't wait to hear from you. If you can give them what they love, you'll become the anomaly they're looking for.

The tools of today are cheaper, easier, and more available than before. If laser focused, you can develop your brand into one that is seen everywhere. From YouTubers to a brick-and-mortar leather shop and all the way to Fortune 500 companies, they all start with finding a problem to solve and then build a brand around it.

Many think a brand is a series of logos and colors, a mission statement, or tagline. But simply put, **a brand is how someone perceives you, what people think you do, and how they feel when they see your company, read your stories, or watch your videos. A brand is about the reaction someone has when they consume what you distribute.** If they love what they consume, you're in a good situation. If not, the earlier you can change those perceptions and feelings the better. What do you think of when you see the name Coca-Cola? What about Apple? Or Nike? Whatever comes to mind for you is the result of decades of hard work by these companies in building their brand.

To know what your brand could be, you first need to understand what you're best at. What do you love to do? Is that something you truly love and dream about, or do you just think it's cool? In the next chapter, you'll learn how to find your niche (or calling), even if it's screaming in your ears and you can't hear it.

-------------- **Roadmap** --------------

1. Understand the concept of business principles. They're in everything you do. Promise me that you'll adopt what you are about to learn. Email me at zack@startwithhatch.com if you are game.

Chapter 3

FINDING YOUR NICHE AND FIGURING OUT WHERE TO START

Everyone has a voice and wants to be heard or at least appreciated. Whether you're an introvert or extrovert, D, I, S, or C (Dominance, Influence, Steadiness, Conscientiousness) on the DISC scale, or one of the MBTI personalities on Myers–Briggs, we are all someone and want the world to know it. The mediums we choose are those comfortable to us and typically to others similar to us. It's human nature. We feel more comfortable around people that don't judge us or make us feel bad. And when you're building or growing your brand, business, or personality, people who appreciate you will flock to you.

But how do you figure out who you are? You may already have an idea of what you can offer to the world, or what you're best at. Start by thinking about where you spend your time or what you search most for online. Consider what you think about, talk about, and dream about. Are those answers something you love? Something that makes you feel good? Or are they just experiences you want to try?

Does the title in your resume exude something you enjoy doing? It's a serious question and one that you need to think about before starting or continuing on this journey. This is going to be tough. If you walk down a path you're not passionate about, you may build a following, but you'll be miserable at the end of the day.

If you're in the exploration phase, think about documenting everything you do for the next week. The food you eat, the conversations you have, what articles you read, what you watch on Netflix, and what you search for online. Create a spreadsheet (or use the template at AnomalyMethod.com) to track how much time you spend on each and how you feel engaging in each activity. Place a number 1 to 4 next to the activity ranking how you feel, 1 being low and 4 being high. At the end of a week you'll have a general idea of what you do during an average week. Don't force your answers to make them seem one way instead of the truth. That will not do anything positive for you. You want to be as accurate as possible with what currently holds your time and attention.

Oftentimes it's shocking how much more time we have in our lives than we think. A binge of a hit TV series, consuming hours of online content, sleeping ten hours a night, or hanging out at a bar multiple nights of the week could be the wake-up call that your time is more poorly spent than you originally thought. This task is not to make you feel bad about yourself but designed to show you where you're spending your time, efforts, and talents.

After seven days, review the document and break it down into categories of sleeping, eating, content consumption, content creation, family, friends, working, and exercising. There are most likely others, but this is a template to get started. Now look at your rankings or feelings under each of these. Are you getting closer to seeing when you're happy and when you're not? Take your content consumption and creation categories and break down which content you enjoyed and which you didn't. When trying to figure out what you love to do, it's likely right in front of you, but you may not see it or know how to make a living from it.

Let's say that while reviewing your stats you realize you love roller coasters. You dream about riding them and you're intrigued with how they work. You love the thrill that amusement parks offer and would love to find ways to make a career out of it, some way, somehow.

Inventory of Your Life

	Sun	Mon	Tue	Wed	Thu	Fri	Sat
1:00am	Sleep	Sleep	Sleep	Sleep	Sleep	Sleep	Sleep
2:00am							
3:00am							
4:00am							
5:00am							
6:00am							
7:00am							
8:00am		Get Ready	Get Ready	Get Ready	Get Ready	Get Ready	
9:00am		Commute	Commute	Commute	Commute	Commute	
10:00am							
11:00am	TV	Work	Work	Work	Work	Work	TV
12:00pm	Out to Lunch						
1:00pm							
2:00pm	Gym						
3:00pm							Gym
4:00pm	TV						
5:00pm	Dinner						
6:00pm		Commute	Commute	Commute	Commute	Commute	TV
7:00pm	TV	Gym	Dinner	Gym	Dinner	Dinner	
8:00pm		Dinner		Dinner			Dinner
9:00pm			TV		TV		
10:00pm		TV		TV		Party	TV
11:00pm	Sleep	Sleep	Sleep	Sleep	Sleep		Sleep
12:00am							

Or, perhaps you're a parent who answers a lot of questions for newer parents through online forums and meetups in your local community. You love helping new parents get results with their families.

It could be that after a lifelong career of recreational swimming you become a head coach of a swim team after realizing you aren't passionate about being a swimmer but coaching others and helping them learn the skills you have developed over the years.

You take a lot of images on your iPhone and see that you're on Instagram and Dribbble seeking inspiration and education. You love images of antique photography and regularly take pictures and post them yourself.

As you begin understanding what you love to do and the complementary skills you possess, you move toward finding your niche. You're finding what makes you unique. If you're not happy in your current career, do some soul-searching. Ask yourself if you're unhappy with your surroundings, or if your job is wrong for you.

This may seem unimportant but having a passion in what you do is one of the number one qualities that helps others flock to you and follow you on your journey to becoming an anomaly.

It's vital to understand who your customer is, but let's not put the cart before the horse—before becoming a customer, they're a prospect or a target customer.

-------------- Roadmap --------------

1. What do you love?
2. Where do you spend your time? Take an inventory of your next seven days and rank them 1 to 4 on how you enjoy them (1 being low, 4 being high).
3. Break down your week and determine where you spend your time and what you love doing.
4. Define your niche.

Chapter 4

WHO IS YOUR
TARGET CUSTOMER?

Brands spend billions a year using the shotgun approach of spraying their message and praying someone will call or reach out to their company. It's effective to learn who your target customer is and reach out to them directly, especially when you're just getting started.

Who is your audience and what do they need? **The process of learning as much about a person or business as you can is the definition of target customer research.** Picture this: You're a CrossFitter, vegan, stay-at-home female athlete, but you receive advertisements for men's work boots. Seems odd, and it is. All too often brands and personalities are targeting their customers completely wrong. They're wasting time and money trying to get attention from people who will never become their customers.

There are people around you right now primed and ready to become your customer. I like to call this low-hanging fruit. Some of these people you likely already know. Someone somewhere is looking for you and what you have to offer. It's up to you to figure out who and where they are. Your target customer is someone who meets a series of criteria that you determine from dissecting your current customer base. If you don't have a current base, you'll make some predictions and edit as you gain more information. This is called a customer pivot.

Standard demographics such as age, gender, height, weight, and race can be used, but it's harder to use only those. Look for a deeper understanding with things like where they vacation, what they eat, where they went to school, brands they wear, where they live, what they like and follow on social media, what language they speak, and how adventurous they are.

If you sign up for a Winc membership (a fantastic wine of the month club), you're asked a series of questions in order to better understand your palate. Questions range from, "How do you like your coffee?" and "Would you jump out of an airplane?" to "What are your favorite fruits?" and whether or not you like steak, scallops, or spicy food. These questions help them better understand you to provide you with wine you're more likely to enjoy. What's stopping you from doing this with your brand in order to provide your customers with the products, services, or content that will most resonate with them? Nothing.

Let's say you have a sample size of 1,000 current followers or customers. That's not a bad-size list. It's one that could provide you with some financial success if you took a little time and energy to better understand who they are. You can do this by creating a poll or survey with targeted questions based on what you need to know about them. You can poll your network through a Facebook post, LinkedIn Group question, or even through an email to your network with a series of questions. You'll also want to get standard data like college level completed, age, gender, and race. You may learn that one demographic is an overwhelming majority of your customer base, and you can create marketing campaigns that speak to those trends.

Knowing your target customer is a multistep process. You need to know: Who are they? What do they look like? Where can I find them? and What appeals to them? If you don't answer all four of these, you'll miss out on key information and likely never convert any of them into customers.

There are lots of ways you can start learning about your target customers. You can leverage your personal network and survey or interview a select group of people who you believe fit the bill of your target customer. By doing this you're getting direct one-to-one knowledge as to what their pain points and problems are. **A pain point or problem is the challenge your prospect is currently experiencing.**

It could be as simple as needing groceries delivered from the grocery store, or as complex as a serious health issue. The problem doesn't matter. What matters is if you can solve their problem and create a relationship, or if you can't, help them find someone else who can.

If you have a solution they're looking for, you can start putting them into your sales funnel, which we will go into more detail about in a later section.

Compile a list of assumptions of what you think the problem is, and then create surveys asking questions around those problems. Send it out to the list you have compiled. Collect all of their data from the surveys and paste it into a spreadsheet. As you progress with your target customers, ask if you can update them on what you're working on.

With every person you have a conversation with, ask if there's someone else that you could be talking to. Maybe they know someone else that fits your target customer profile. This could be called a referral, but since you're not selling anything yet, it's more of a warm lead. A warm lead indicates that the person has either shown interest, or someone has informed you that they may be a good fit. A cold lead means the person has shown no sign of interest, and you're just testing the waters. If they say yes, ask how you should contact the new person or group.

Let's say you create a marketing and branding set for one demographic, but then learn that you were wrong, or something changes with that demographic and it's no longer your target customer. Any marketing that you were using should be edited or removed as it'll be speaking to someone you have proven is not a good fit.

Now that you have a better understanding of how to consume *Anomaly,* you'll be taken through three parts: Understanding the Sales Funnel, Becoming the Anomaly, and Anomalies in the Wild. Understanding the Sales Funnel will detail why it takes multiple steps to get the results you desire. Becoming the Anomaly details techniques that get amazing results. Finally, Anomalies in the Wild walks you through case studies of individuals and companies who have become an anomaly by using specific tools and/or mediums.

-------------- **Roadmap** --------------

1. Determine your target audience/customer using standard demographics like age, gender, race, annual income, plus deep demographics like where

they hang out, how they speak, what do they like, where do they spend money, what do they drive, where did they go to school, etc.

2. What are three unique identifiers of your target customer?
3. What challenges or pain points do your targets have?
4. What type of questions are they asking you?
5. Select 5 to 10 keywords and key phrases that your targets use in their vernacular and what they search online. Don't get cute.

Chapter 5

THE SALES FUNNEL

A sales funnel is the process of taking a visitor or prospect through your system from first view to conversion. It typically takes somewhere between five to seven positive interactions to land a qualified client. Why waste your time with cold-calling if there's a good chance the answer is no? By following the sales funnel, you can save yourself a lot of time and energy as well as get the conversion you're striving for.

Let's take a look at an example using a five- to seven-step funnel. Once you understand what a funnel is and its contents, we will go over free or cheap ways to get prospects into your funnel. How cheap? Roughly the price of an Extra Value Meal at McDonald's. That's cheap! The seven steps to this sales funnel are:

Step 1: Bringing Awareness
Step 2: Getting Contact Information
Step 3: The Follow-Up
Step 4: Dig Deep
Step 5: Hard Sell

Step 6: 24-Hour Follow-Up
Step 7: Ongoing Support

Some studies show it takes up to 20 positive interactions to make a conversion. A positive interaction doesn't mean you have serviced or sold anything in a positive way to the client. It means they've had some sort of favorable interaction with you, even if it's seeing the business card you left them. On the opposite end of things, if your potential client has a negative interaction with you, it takes up to 35 positive reactions to regain credibility. And sometimes, you may have lost them for life no matter how many positive interactions you have with them. So, make sure all of your interactions with potential clients are positive! It's key to note that typically you will not promote or talk sales with anyone until Step 5. Knowing that it takes several steps to convert a prospect into a customer, why would you try to sell on the first interaction? You already know it won't work. Instead, create a relationship. A relationship similar to one with a new friend.

Close your eyes and think about the last time you got a cold call from a salesman. Most likely you were not delighted to get the call and were probably more on the irritated side. So why would you want to do that to your potential customers? Instead, find a different path so that you can introduce yourself, educate them, and make them fall in love with you all before you pitch your product, services, or whatever you're selling. Use the sales funnel as a guide or template, adjusting the material and message over time with your customer base.

It may sound simple, but if you follow this process your deal flow won't only increase, but your bottom-line sales closings will too. Deal flow is the total number of prospects added to your sales funnel. The best part? It doesn't matter what you're selling: an app, a service, a product, or even a date—yes, you can use this process to ask someone out, too. This process increases your bottom line, exposure, website traffic, social media engagement, customers, and leads from customers who have turned into raving fans.

Most people quit after Step 2 in a sales funnel.

Before you develop your sales funnel, define the unit you're tracking—a sale, a subscriber, or interested potential dating partners—so that you have something to track. If you obtain a 2 percent conversion rate, you have a unit to measure. If you don't know what unit to measure, think about the numbers you track the most or data you want to know and start there.

The goal of a sales funnel must be a unit that is quantifiable, as mentioned previously. In most cases that means converting a target customer into a paying one, although if you're building a freemium service, it may be acquiring a user. These freemium service businesses typically run advertising and the "user" never sees a **paywall, which is an arrangement where a website will restrict access to certain pieces of content unless you have paid to access it.** An example of this is ESPN Insider. You can only read Insider content if you're a paying member.

As with anything, it's good practice to track what's working and what's not. If you don't weigh yourself regularly when on a diet, you won't know if that diet is working. In business, if you can't understand why a reaction is happening one way or the other, you can't improve upon it for future endeavors. By putting best business practices into your approach, it'll help you even if you're just running a social media page. If you can understand how people think and how they'll act, you'll have a stronger indication of how to get more conversions. Find a metric that you can track and religiously try to improve it.

The first step of the sales funnel is a hard pill to swallow for some people. You have to provide some sort of free content. Something that can educate someone about your area of expertise or engage them in some way. But, it comes back to the "deposit before you withdraw" idea. In order to get someone started in your sales funnel, you need to hook them in.

------------- Roadmap -------------

1. What metric are you tracking?
2. Create a sales funnel spreadsheet or download the Anomaly Method Roadmap at AnomalyMethod.com and begin to fill it in with contact information data points: name, phone number, email, address, keywords, where you found them, step in sales funnel, conversations had, their interests, their pain points, etc.

Chapter 6

BRINGING AWARENESS

The first step in any funnel is bringing awareness to you and/or your business by getting seen by your potential customers. This can be produced in a variety of ways depending on what you're trying to get out to people. Some of the ways to do this are an introduction by a mutual acquaintance, writing and sharing a blog post, creating and posting a video on YouTube or Vimeo, doing an interview, or making a comment on Quora, Reddit, or other social media posts. Humans see over five thousand different ads every single day. That's an astounding amount. Look around. Look at your clothes, your phone, your car, your office. Ads are everywhere.

Sometimes you can be in the same room, office, event, or online platform and never be seen. We will go over ways to be noticed later. (Hint: My favorite way is the Zack Miller Way.) In the business world, the overwhelming majority looks the same. They wear a suit. I wear jeans and a black T-shirt with black Sambas. It's my uniform, and it helps me stand out.

If you're attending a conference or meetup, get your hands on the attendee list beforehand and reach out to the attendees one by one and let them know that you'll be in the room and would love to meet. This way you have already introduced yourself before you ever meet in person. If they respond, then you have the added validation that they're interested in meeting you as well. The hard part of making the introduction is over, and you haven't even met them in person yet—well done you! The pressure is lessened.

When you meet someone for the first time, don't ask, "So, um, what do you do?" That is unoriginal, boring, and not in the least setting you apart as an anomaly. Instead, ask questions like, "What vacations do you have planned?"; "What's a project that you're working on that you're pumped up about?"; "What are you watching on Netflix?"; or "What do you do when you're not working?" These questions, while fairly nonintrusive, are much more interesting and engaging. People love to talk about what gets them excited and what they're passionate about. Besides being great conversation pieces, what better way to get people to have positive associations with you and/or your business than if you get them talking about those things that make them happy and excited!

When it comes to creating a visible message, you can't do what everyone else is doing. In swimming, Michael Phelps' competitors would often look over to see how far ahead he was, which led Phelps to an advantage. He rarely looked at his competitors and stayed focused on the task at hand. You need to be tunnel-visioned. Set your sights on what you want to accomplish and don't let anything, or anyone, take your attention away from that. Focus on what you can do, not what someone else is doing. Sure, you can see what others are doing to make sure you don't copy them, but to stand out, do what no one else is doing. If you're creating a blog, podcast, or video, don't interview the same people others are, but if you do, don't ask the exact same questions. Ask different questions that provoke new insights into the subject and that benefit your audience.

By the way, standing out doesn't mean you have to be an eyesore or quirky just for the sake of being quirky. Not everyone needs to be a Lady Gaga. To stand out, you can do something as simple as smiling and saying thank you. Those two things are not done enough today.

Find creative ways to stand out. If you host a podcast, try interviewing a guest who doesn't frequently do interviews, or interview a guest in a unique setting. Whichever ways you choose to be creative, the ultimate goal is to get the attention of your target customers. Otherwise, it doesn't matter how creative you are, the content will be useless as no one will ever see it.

When you're on social media or search for a keyword on Google, what makes you stop scrolling? Start a swipe file, a collection of sales and advertisement documents and examples, somewhere on your computer where you can compile everything that made you stop scrolling and start engaging. This will benefit you later.

How can you do something similar for your marketing? Don't copy what someone else is doing. Dissect what they did, why it worked, and how you can put your own spin on it. It could also be finding a meetup that hosts a series of your targets and buying them cupcakes, or if it's at a bar a round of shots. By doing something off the cuff and out of the ordinary, your targets will sit there and say, "Wait, what just happened?"

> At LessConf in Atlanta, GA, one of the sponsors was Blue Ox Jerky, a direct-to-consumer beef jerky business. LessConf founder Allan Branch was looking for more unique items and had tried Blue Ox in the past. He reached out to the company and invited them to sponsor the conference, plus put a sample of their product in front of their attendees. Branch knew his target, and leveraged that information. He learned who Blue Ox was trying to get in front of through a conversation and he saw overlap. He then sold the idea of Blue Ox getting in front of hundreds of prospects in one sitting.

Let's look at another example of how to get new customers interested in you. When you're in the food court at the mall or Costco, what do most of those restaurants and vendors do to get you interested in their food? They give you a free sample! For the minimal cost of giving free samples, they take a small following and turn it into a raving fan base (assuming their food is tasty).

These styles of first engagements show people who you are. And even if your business is not food- or drink-based, food and coffee sell. Want someone's attention? Send them a $5 gift card for a local coffee shop along with a handwritten introduction card. Maybe even invite them out. Go ahead, try it out and see how they react. There's a pretty good chance you'll get the meeting with them.

Once you get someone's attention, you need to validate their fit with what you're offering. A good way to do that is to collect some information from them. If they won't give you their email address, they won't give you their money.

-------------- **Roadmap** --------------

1. Create a list of three go-to icebreaker questions for when you first meet someone.
2. Create a swipe file for marketing examples that hook you.
3. What interests your targets?
4. Provide three free ways to provide value to your targets. Example: Food court samples at shopping mall.

Chapter 7

GET CONTACT INFORMATION

Now that you know several ways to raise awareness of you and/or your business, the next step is to connect with them. But you can't connect if you don't have their contact information. So how do you get this?

Free information is often already produced on your end, it's just hidden. Instead, use your most popular content to excite someone about learning from you and give it to them in exchange for their contact information. If you can get a potential customer to your website or blog, entice them to sign up for free follow-up information. The more they see you as a helper, the more likely they're to become a customer.

If you're meeting someone in person, connecting with them can be as simple as exchanging business cards. Online it could be liking one of their social media pages or subscribing to their email list or YouTube page. You're looking for ways to get their contact information by providing something of value to them, such as your like or subscription. Or that value to them could even be as extensive as an ebook, access to exclusive material, a webinar, an email list, or entering to win some sort

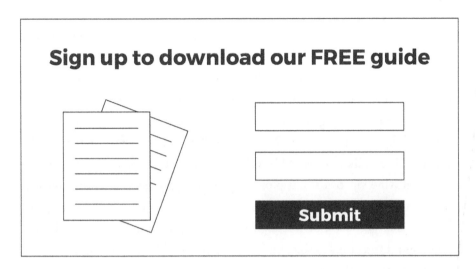

of prize you can give away. Since you know that people don't buy during their first meeting, by receiving their contact information it allows you to play the game of follow-up.

Again, don't go for the big sell on the first move. That would be like going in for a steamy smooch 10 minutes into the first date. First, you have to meet the potential customer or get them to your online page. Tease them a little and then get their contact information or have them subscribe. A way you can do this is to offer a free piece of content in exchange for their name and email.

As mentioned earlier, over 80 percent of people get to Step 2 of the sales funnel. They bring awareness to themselves and/or their business, and they exchange some sort of contact information. But only 20 percent get to Step 3.

If you're still confused about sales funnels, think of them this way: When a prospect goes through each step of the sales funnel, you increase your chances to boost your conversion rate. You learn more about them, who they are, what their pain points are, and if you're even a good fit to help them solve their problems. Having applicable data guides your conversations with your prospects. The more you know, the more likely you are to make a solid pitch and have educated communications with your prospect so that they go from being a prospect to a customer, ready and waiting with their credit card, Apple Pay, or even Bitcoin to pay you for your products or services.

No one continues to engage in something they don't like or receive value from. They'll stick around if they feel they're receiving value from you. Eventually you'll get to the point where it's intuitive for someone to say, "I've been helped so much I kind of have to pay for this." That is what we are trying to get to—the point where they can't say no. Gary Vaynerchuk, popular businessman and Internet guru, talks about a rule where you always want to be giving 51 percent versus the other person's 49 percent. Giving more than you take up front and staying patient benefits you in the long run. Vaynerchuk grew his families wine business from $3 million annually to $60 million. One of his techniques was when YouTube first came out, he recorded wine videos of him providing his feedback and knowledge on wine. He did this by simply recording a video and uploading to YouTube, nothing fancy. He knew his customers were looking for knowledge on wine and took advantage of a medium that not many were on yet and capitalized his knowledge of wine and shared it with the world. Vaynerchuk now is one of the top social media influencers in the world.

While ebooks seem like a lot of trouble, you may already have the content written. All you need to do is package it. If you have a creative team member, have them turn your copy into an ebook. And guess what? An ebook doesn't have to be as long as a physical book, and most of the time they're not. They can range anywhere from a few pages to a few hundred, but there's no standard or quota you have to meet. It's whatever length is needed to educate your reader and prove your point.

There are many tools that you can use to create a call to action, even ones for free like Sumo. Sumo uses techniques to entice visitors to provide their contact information in exchange for educational information. They then pair the information from Sumo to your email marketing platform in which your supporter would then automatically deliver the material the call to action said it would. We will do a deep dive on all of this in a later chapter.

A lead magnet is a form of call to action driven by a link or image that points to the offer. As a visitor hovers over and clicks the offer, a new page or pop-up grabs their contact information and sends it to your email marketing platform. If technology scares you, or you're a newbie, these tools have become easy to use.

If you don't have a creative team member on your staff, you can use cheap design tools like Canva, or hire someone at Fiverr to help you. Decades ago these tools didn't exist, or if they did, they were expensive and difficult to use. Now, they're a couple of bucks and easy to use. All of these tools, and many more, are used primarily during the second step of the sales funnel.

Once someone gives you their data, you're one step closer to turning them into a customer, subscriber, or follower. Next, you need to double down on the value you can provide for them.

-------------- **Roadmap** --------------

1. Create a call-to-action plan for in-person networking and online (i.e., convert a series of blog posts into an ebook that can be downloaded by the visitor in return for their contact information).

Chapter 8

THE FOLLOW-UP

Step 3 is to follow up and provide value.

Once you have a prospect or new relationship and a means to contact them, you're at Step 3. It's one of the most important steps in your funnel. It's the follow-up, where you provide additional value and supplemental information.

How many times have you met someone new, signed up for an email list or subscribed to a newsletter, and never received anything after? I'd be willing to bet that a large percentage of the people you meet at networking events never contact you afterward. People get lazy, they think the contact information alone is the gold mine. Sorry, it's not.

I wanted to test this assumption. I host a TV show for ABC in my area, Norfolk-Virginia Beach, VA. I attended a local networking group and pitched who I was to the group of seventy-five. Mind you, these seventy-five people were target customers for me. Since the number one question I am asked is how to get more customers, visitors, leads, exposure, or revenue, I provided something of significant value. I told the group, "I would love to have each of you on my TV show free of charge to promote your business and let the area know who you are and what you do! Please reach out to me so we can schedule."

Think about this for a second, seventy-five prospects in a room and I can provide them each with more exposure. How many do you think reached out to me? You'll probably be as shocked as I was to find out that not a single one contacted me to take me up on this offer. Not one of those seventy-five became the anomaly. They missed out on an opportunity to get in front of my 25,000 weekly viewers. Not to mention all of the additional marketing that could have been done for the coming years by continued promotions.

How do you make sure your follow-up is strong? While connecting with your prospect, take a mental note about the topics you discussed, or immediately following your interactions take a note on the back of their business card or add it to the notes section of their contact profile in your phone. The key here is to remember the topics you discussed so you can mention it later. It's not the topic that matters but making sure you have a solid conversation with them and can recall its highlights. As mentioned earlier, most of the time it's better if you start by creating a relationship.

Here's an example: If while talking with your prospective client they mentioned they wanted to improve their copywriting skills, take time to research some of the top copywriting tips and follow up with a simple email message.

Subject Line:
Hey, Nice to meet you
Body:
Their Name,

*It was awesome to meet you at XYZ event. I am glad we were able to chat about (recap the conversation). You had mentioned you were looking to improve your copywriting skills. When I got back to my office, I did some research and found (**insert link on topic**) this article. I thought it might be helpful.*

Have a great day,
Your Name

Yes. It's that simple. Emails should be short, sweet, and to the point. How short? Write your email text message length. They're mobile, reading on the run, and have zero interest in TL;DR (Too Long; Didn't Read). If you read your message and say, "Wow, this is a lot," reread it and make sure you don't overwhelm them. Now, there's a time and place for a longer, more detailed email, but not at this point in the sales funnel. Keep it simple and to the point.

More often than not, this will create new conversations between you and your prospects and that is exactly what you want to happen. Creating a relationship with as many people as you can is a strong strategy to succeed in business (and life), because the more people you know, the more potential for opportunities to come your way.

It's important to follow up with a new contact within 24 hours in order to get that relationship moving forward. If you promised a visitor on your website something from your call to action in Step 2, get it to them in less than 24 hours. You can do it manually by receiving a notification, but it's a lot easier now to automate the process. Once they opt-in or agree to provide their contact information in exchange for your offer, you can have your email marketing platform do everything for you. As you get started, there are many free versions of email marketing platforms. As you grow your email list or add additional contacts to the list, the pricing goes up, but if you're following these steps and turn your new prospects into customers, you should be able to afford the increase in costs.

The worst thing you can do is obtain a visitor, get them to opt-in, and never send them what you promised. Once the visitor subscribes, send the material immediately to their email inbox. Ideally, you'll have this step automated, so you don't even have to think about it.

A tool built to help visitors talk to a human (or sometimes a robot, scary!) is a chat box, which can be automatically added to your site. They trigger when a visitor takes a specific action, like spends an extended period of time on your site or clicks on three pages. The chat box pops up and asks if your visitor has any questions.

In the real world, this is similar to shopping in a retail environment and having an employee see you and say, "Hello." They probe to see what you're looking for or if there's something they can help you with.

Most of these online techniques are simply in-person concepts with a digital twist. How annoying is it to search a website for a specific link and you can't find it? The chat box helps, since the person running it knows the answer. It's a tool that helps you communicate directly with your audience to learn what they're looking for. The next time you go to a website and get hit with one of these actions, you'll know that you're in someone's Step 2.

The point to realize is that it doesn't matter how many leads, prospects, or potential clients for which you have contact information. If you don't follow up, then nothing is going to happen. Period.

-------------- **Roadmap** --------------

1. Follow up with everyone you meet. No questions asked.
2. Collect notes on the conversations you have with new relationships.

Chapter 9

DIG DEEP

Now that you have brought awareness to your brand, provided some free content, and done a follow-up with your prospect, it's time to dig deep. This is important because getting accurate information to analyze is critical, as you need to understand the problem your prospect has that you're trying to solve. You're also trying to find out if you're even the best fit to solve their problem.

During your questioning and research if you find that a relationship is not mutually beneficial, or you can't solve their problem, don't leave them hanging. Refer them to someone who could be a great fit and even arrange an introduction. This goes a long way in the business world because it shows the prospect that you don't just want their business, but you genuinely want to help them. And when someone feels like you went above and beyond to help them, they won't often forget that. There's a greater chance of them referring people to you in the future. Business is about networking and relationships, so build strong relationships!

If you do find that you can provide a solution to the prospect's problem, then you're on to Step 4 of your sales funnel. Understanding a prospect's needs, or problem, is critical to helping you prepare a pitch that produces the return you want, whether that be a sale, a subscriber, or whatever unit you're measuring. In Step 4, you're going to ask your prospect questions such as, "Anything keeping you up at night?" or "What's one thing you want to do in your business?"

The latter question is taking the time to learn about bucket-list items of your prospect. It doesn't matter what their answer is, you can respond with, "What's holding you back from doing x, y, or z?" Whatever their answer is will provide enormous insight into how you can best service their needs.

The key to Step 4 is to really understand if the pain point is major or minor. Depending on your pricing, the higher the price, the higher the pain point needs to be. On a scale of 1 to 10, if a problem costs 10 and its customer views it as a 1, what's the likelihood of them buying?

Let's use an example of a red light coming on in your vehicle. What do you do? You call the mechanic and schedule an appointment to figure out what's wrong with your car. They give it a look and say that either it's a timing belt and costs $50, or it's an engine issue that costs $5,000. One of those is a much bigger issue than the other. A 100 times increase in price makes someone think about their answer significantly more—unless money is not an issue.

Let's say you have a toothache. You call your dentist and schedule a visit. They take a look and say you have a cavity. Your insurance will cover $200 of the $1,000 procedure, and it'll take three hours to perform. With this answer you have two pain points, the additional cost and the time commitment.

There are several creative ways that you can gather the information you need, including a Facebook Poll, surveys sent out to your existing following, through a "Contact Us" link, by analyzing the data from the content people consume, or by simply picking up the phone and engaging in a conversation. In a later chapter you'll learn about 50-Ten, a creative challenge and way to engage with several prospects over their pain points.

If you've made to this step, you're in good shape. You have gotten their attention, they've given you some information about themselves, you have identified a problem or hole they need fixed, and you're another step closer to converting them at the end of your funnel. It's time for the sale.

-------------- **Roadmap** --------------

1. Determine what your prospects pain points are by asking them "What's keeping you up at night?" Ask them to rank it 1 to 4.

2. Create three strategies to learn about your prospects (i.e., "Contact Us" form on your website).

Chapter 10

HARD SELL

Step 5 is where you put everything together and go for the sell. For suspense, let's call it the hard sell. The hard sell varies from business to business and depends upon the metric you're tracking. If your metric is subscribers, then the hard sell for you will be simply asking them to subscribe to your channel. Or perhaps you have a website project for which you need to raise money. Your hard sell will be asking people to fund your project.

It's important to note that you need to stay consistent in the way you communicate. For example, if you were always emailing back and forth, don't send over a proposal on Twitter. As crazy as it may seem, people will take their prospects for a ride on the "Where should I send this?" wheel. Don't do that. This process can already be complex enough, don't add to it unnecessarily.

However you communicate with your prospect, recap every moment you have had with them. This is a time where it's okay to be thorough and lengthy. You want to remind them how much time you have already invested in them. This is a good time to remind them of the results you have already produced for them. Make this quantifiable. Seeing a single quantifiable improvement on the metric most important to your prospect is critical to get them to stay with you.

They can "see" the progress, which gets them excited about continuing to work with you.

Let's take a minute to talk about conversion rates. **A conversion rate is the percentage of visitors you turn into customers.** The goal is always to increase your conversion rate. By using a series of steps, like a sales funnel, to meet, educate, and help others first, you're improving your chances of increasing your conversion rate, instead of pushing a sales pitch down someone's throat during an initial meeting. If you have 100 visitors at Step 1 in the funnel and convert five into customers by Step 5, you have a 5 percent conversion rate. These rates vary depending on the type of business or response you seek. There are plenty of businesses whose conversion rates are industry leading, yet are only technically a 1 percent conversion rate.

The same goes for you. Find guides that you can use like this sales funnel template and see how you can incorporate them into your brand. You need to find ways to stand out, but in many cases a guide is the same process over and over. It doesn't change, there may be a few options, but the process is simple. Say you're getting a business license. The process is similar city to city. Some applications may ask for different questions, but for the most part it's just a way to do it. There's nothing creative involved. To grow, find where others have created guides for you to follow while putting your slant on it where applicable. Obviously, on a business license there's nothing you can do other than filling out the form, but if you were to apply for a business plan competition, you can get creative and show why you're different.

If you're getting out of college and looking for a job, sorry, almost every job application or resume looks the same. What can you do to put your spin on it? If you look the same as everyone else, you won't stand out. You'll almost always get overlooked, even if you have the best ability, talent, and skills required. Think about creating a compelling video resume explaining why you're a good fit for the position. Become the anomaly. When you get a prospect to the position of the hard sell, you have put them through the steps. They understand you and now you can provide more value with a paid account.

YouTubers often have premium accounts where paid users get bonus content. Their entire subscriber list consumes hours of content. Slowly and methodically they put them through a process without the viewer even knowing it. Netflix creates bingeable content and you don't realize you spent your entire weekend watching a series. They create desirable content that hooks you. Even when they raise their price or ask you to pay for something else, you don't even sweat it. You just do it.

Amazon does the same with Prime and its more than 65 million subscribers. Not just Amazon, which is free to view, but their Prime service makes it easy for a customer to get free and speedy delivery on almost anything. If you help people and make them want you, the price will almost never matter. They become obsessed with your content. The process seems a little ridiculous. You may be thinking, "You want me to not sell to my customer when I meet them?" No, I don't. I want you to create a relationship that takes them through a path and makes them treat you like a Netflix binge.

If you follow these steps, when you get to the hard sell and have a binger, you'll be satisfied with the results. But your relationship with your audience should never end at the sale. Once you make your pitch, whether they bite or not, you should follow up with them quickly.

TIP: Most people receive a paycheck somewhere around the 1st and 15th of every month. Around those same times of the month the average person has some sort of rent or mortgage, or other large bills due. If you try to do your hard sell around those dates and don't get a good response, think about changing the dates you try to around the 7th and 22nd of every month. You may have a better chance of conversion.

-------------- **Roadmap** --------------

1. Document everything with your prospect and provide them the proposal or conversion that you are tracking.
2. Update your sales funnel document with your results.

Chapter 11

24-HOUR FOLLOW-UP

No matter if you succeeded with the hard sell or not, it's imperative to follow up within 24 hours. If someone bought or converted on the metric you're tracking, send a text or email message, or phone them, letting them know their product or service is under way. Confirmation and a simple thank you goes a long way.

If they signed up for an app, send them an onboard message that answers frequently asked questions, along with a step-by-step playbook on how to use your platform to its maximum ability. Always have a personalized piece to messages, even if they're automated, and ask for users or customers to reply if they have any questions. This builds confidence in the product or service you're now providing for them. Many of the automation tools that are recommended in *Anomaly* have ways that you can send a personalized message.

As frustrating as it can be, there will be times you'll follow these steps to a T and won't get the results you want. Rest assured, it's most likely that it's just not the right time for them to purchase your product or service. If it's not that, then it's probably the cost of your product or service. At that point, it's up to you if you want to lower your rates to cater to them or stick with what you believe it's worth.

You can also keep the prices the same but offer a payment plan. Don't give up on your prospects. You have worked hard to create a relationship with them and until they tell you "We are not interested," keep them in a longer funnel. Over the next few weeks or months, send them ongoing educational material or content that is relevant to them based on your funnel research.

Just because someone doesn't buy, doesn't mean they're not interested. Dig deeper to see what has them on the fence. They may be wondering: Can you really help them? What results will they see? Can they really trust you? Is the product really what they need? Can it fix their problems? Can they afford it?

These are all probing questions you can learn from. Use them in future conversations and in your literature online and throughout your website. Don't abandon the relationship. Continue providing value and keep them engaged. It's even more important to keep providing value if you did get the hard sell since they've now become your customers. There are several ways to do this through ongoing support.

-------------- **Roadmap** --------------

1. Follow up within 24 hours to ensure your prospect has everything they need and is satisfied.
2. If the answer was no, probe to find out why. Document on sales funnel spreadsheet.
3. If the answer was yes, probe to find out why. Document on sales funnel spreadsheet.

Chapter 12

ONGOING SUPPORT

O nce you have turned a visitor or prospect into a customer, you want to keep them around, engaged, and happy for as long as possible. Whether it's an app, service, product, tool, or something else, if you sell them once and keep them excited and engaged, there's an excellent chance you'll be able to sell them on future items. They'll also share their experience with their network and you'll gain more deal flow into your sales funnel. Do this through ongoing support and personalized messages. These can be things like handwritten cards, new features, informational case studies pertaining to their field or interests, or additional releases of your product for them to use or buy.

Just like in Step 6, if they don't buy it's not the end of the world. It happens. In fact, 67.45 percent of online shopping carts are abandoned before the customer completes a sale. Every ecommerce shop online has dealt with this issue at one time or another. What makes you think you won't? Take a play out of Amazon's book and send your prospect a reminder of what they put in their "cart," or provide them additional ways to use the product or describe how a specific customer of yours is seeing tremendous success using your product or service. You never know what will make your prospect finally say yes. Sometimes, it's the oddest things and at the strangest times.

The last thing you want to do is quit on someone who could be a serious customer. Meet Edgar, a social media scheduling tool, does this by sending out a weekly newsletter to both those who are already members and to those who subscribe. The content they share is a mixture of their own content on topics their viewers are searching for typically around best practices on social media or algorithm changes on the different social media platforms. For paying members, they send out a weekly "how you're doing" email chronicling how your content is doing against the previous week. They understand that their viewers are searching for specific content. Instead of letting them go elsewhere to find it, they poll their viewers through surveys and questions throughout their social media channels to learn what they're searching for. They analyze the data to determine what content they should create. They then share it throughout their vehicles, social media channels, and through a weekly email wrap-up. In the email, they throw in a call to action to sign up for their products. They know that if their viewers have been following along for a while receiving content and potentially going through the steps of the funnel that a number of them will click the bait and sign up.

An example of awesome ongoing support is Best Self, who produces a top-selling journal for people to be productive, hit their goals, and succeed. With an endorsement from Daymond John, *Self Journal* is one of the most popular journals on the market. Although they're a business without a plethora of products in their product line, they do employ a weekly Motivational Newsletter which is one part inspirational and one part educational. They walk subscribers through best practices, ways to use their products, what they're working on, and customer stories.

Each week thousands get their newsletter, which helps their customers better use their products. Very little of their newsletter is advertising new products. By continuing to share how to use their products better and ways that others have used their products, they create raving fans who do actually wake up thinking about their products because they have to physically use their journals every day. Journaling can be difficult for some as it takes creating a habit to get used to following a process. Best Self provides an FAQ section on ways to get into a habit, stay on a habit, and to produce a better life. By sending a weekly email, you're teaching your following to expect something, and if you're really good at it, your following will even look forward to getting your newsletter.

By setting someone's expectations of when a piece of content will be available, you're bettering your chances of them searching for, opening, and engaging with your material. If you say you're going to provide content at a certain time or on a specific path, don't miss that time as your viewers will tune in and be disappointed. By training your following to expect your content, they can also share, recommend, and talk with their friends afterward about what you produced. Similar to a sports game, if your content is talk worthy, your fans will want to Tweet about it, share it on Facebook, email their friends, and discuss it around the watercooler at work.

Having a well-thought-out sales funnel is essential to the growth of your brand. Each step needs to be planned out and tested. Once you have the funnel built, it's time to fill it up!

-------------- **Roadmap** --------------

1. Create a schedule for ongoing marketing through content such as a weekly newsletter.

PART 2

BECOMING THE ANOMALY

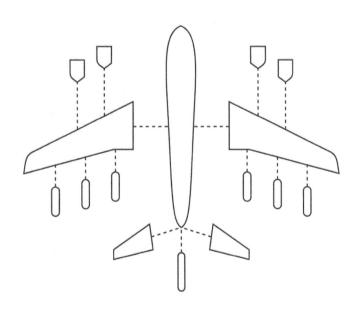

Chapter 13

INVENTORY

Content is king. The world you live in now is not only filled with thousands of ads a day, but with tons upon tons of content. **Content is information like blog posts, videos, infographics, podcasts, how-to guides, walkthroughs, etc.** Some of that content you love to consume, and others not so much. Content is what you search for on Google and then read about. It's what you see as you scroll on social media feeds. It's found in video clips on YouTube and in the conversations you have with your friends and target customers. As much as you may like to think you're the only one providing the content pertaining to your expertise, think again. People search everywhere for new content to educate them, help them, and provide them value. However, don't be discouraged one bit! It doesn't matter if someone else is already creating content around your topics or industry, *your content* is different because it's from *your point of view.*

Now that you understand the sales funnel and what it entails, it's time to take an inventory of the content you already have. Whether you have little to no content, or have it coming out of your ears, the key is to start with what you have. There's no reason to put in the time and effort to re-create a piece of content if it already exists and you would just be mimicking it. As with anything, be aware of what you already have, and then evaluate what's working and what's not. You may have a useful piece of content that needs to be made accessible. Your best content should be given away and heavily promoted. That means getting it in front of a variety of target customers. If you hide your best work, it could be one of the only reasons you're being held back from reaching your goals.

Take inventory of your work and network. This begins by finding all of the content you have ever produced and then putting it into a spreadsheet. Use descriptors like titles or headlines, keywords, tags, categories, target customer produced for, and/or date of release to organize and classify your pieces. On the network spreadsheet, look at your contacts' information and create columns with name, email, how you know them, what they do, and any other pertinent information to help you identify whether or not they may be a target customer. You're doing this to know where you stand and to see which relationships you already have, what content you have created, what content is working, and which group of people is engaging with that content. If you have no content, don't worry, you at least have relationships. These are just as important because you can position yourself to help them with exposure, answer their questions, and understand what content they're requiring.

Not all content you produce gets the results you're looking for and that is okay. You'll learn far more from your trials than you will from your successes. Content takes time and sometimes what looks promising ends up being lackluster.

First, evaluate your content. What do you have? On which topics? How long are they? How many people have seen them? Once you have an idea of where you are now, you'll be able to see where you need to go. What holes can you fill? Where is your content lacking? What other kinds of content can you get into?

A lot of gurus talk about producing content over and over and you'll do awesome. Heck, that's part of what we're talking about here in *Anomaly*. What they rarely say is that your content can't suck. That doesn't mean the content has to be the best produced. What matters is providing quality content. Are people engaging with your content by liking, commenting, and sharing consistently? The best content gets people talking.

 22,523 Likes    861 Shares    1,711 Comments

If you have quality content, does it matter if the production quality is high? No. Does it possibly get you more responses and a better following if it is? Absolutely. As you get better at producing and your bank account grows, you can invest in higher-quality equipment or even a production company or writer to help you polish up your content. But at the root of it all, the most important thing is producing content people crave and engage with. So, how do you know if you're producing this kind of content? This can be difficult to gauge, especially if your following is small or doesn't respond.

Let's say your analytics show people are consuming or viewing your content, but there's a lack of engagement from your visitors. **Engagement is the act of response to your content through a message, share, or a visible way to track your content's interaction.** To increase exposure and learn more about how your content is perceived, poll or survey your followers to see what they think of the content. You can even do it anonymously for a more genuine answer. This will be difficult to receive. No one likes to hear how and where they're not measuring up. But, you need to get clarity and, if your content sucks, you need to learn why. Then you can fix it and get it back into the hands of those who said it was weak to see if you successfully changed it.

If your content is poor, it'll be next to impossible to be successful. Your content has to be awesome. And if you have awesome content and have done awesome things, don't be afraid to show it off! If you don't put yourself in the spotlight, no one else will do it for you.

------------- Roadmap -------------

1. Create a content spreadsheet, use titles or headlines, keywords, tags, categories, target customer produced for, and/or date of release or download at AnomalyMethod.com. What content has better results? Rank 1 to 4. What medium has the best results? Rank 1 to 4.

2. Go through all the content that you have created and the mediums in which you post it to and add it to the spreadsheet.

3. Create a network spreadsheet using columns with name, email, how you know them, what they do, any other pertinent information, and if they

could be a target customer or download at AnomalyMethod.com. Who is more influential than others? Rank 1 to 4.

Chapter 14

PROMOTING YOURSELF
IS NOT BEING COCKY

t's a wonderful feeling when a brand receives a boost in exposure. If you can be featured in a publication or interviewed on a popular podcast, you're getting in front of a new group of people. (We'll talk more later in the book about how to make this happen.) The results give you more website traffic, added subscriptions to your email list, more phone calls, and more sales. There's a period right after you get featured when people start noticing you. It's exciting. You're finally getting the attention you deserve and worked hard for. Then a few days go by and people move on to something else. What can you do once the honeymoon phase of exposure wears off? It happens fast! There are ways you can keep that excitement alive over the following weeks, months, and years to leverage those past opportunities.

Once you have exposure, you want it to be seen more than once and shared repeatedly. This is where most brands mess up. They get the recognition but never leverage it. They never promote it after the fact, and it sits in the pit of misery never to be seen again. Let's say you receive an article written about you in a popular magazine. That popular magazine boasts 250,000 monthly readers, of which a large portion see your story. This is wonderful. But then what? The magazine doesn't promote your story the following month since they need to get eyeballs on their new content. So, you must take control and market this story yourself. Wait for them and it may never happen again. All too often, amazing stories are produced and the producer of the content promotes the story once and then it never is marketed again.

As you grow your brand, the goal is that your network is growing with it. Imagine gaining 100 new followers a month. At the end of the year you would have 1,200 new followers. If you promoted that content in January and only in January, 1,100 new followers would miss out. Do you get why recycling your content is important now? Since it takes six times for someone to be seen the first time anyway, get it out of your head that everyone who is following you always sees what you're producing.

Becoming an anomaly means you're seen a lot. So much so that your brand is recognizable, and you begin to hear people say, "We see you everywhere. How do you do that?"

We have 24 hours in a day, and what you do with it sets you apart. Anomalies don't waste time or complain, they are focus-driven and maximize their time. Instead of having a series of one-on-one meetings where you only get your message out to the person or small group, think about taking that exact same content and create it using a medium in which you can share it with everyone, like a video or podcast. Besides reaching numerous people at once, if those people feel you have provided them value, then they now have an easy way to share that content.

A 1,000-subscriber email list that has an open rate of 25 percent is missing 75 percent of its subscribers. You must continue to promote and leverage your wins no matter how old they are. The content inside of them may no longer be relevant but that doesn't matter. What does matter is leveraging your brand, leveraging the platform of that popular magazine by saying, "Featured in *Popular Magazine*" in your messaging. This is what sports teams do. They promote when they won, not when they lost. When was the last time you heard the Tampa Bay Buccaneers talk about the year they lost almost every game? You don't. You hear them promote when they won the Super Bowl. Even if it was decades ago, it shows that they're champions. What big wins do you already have? What brands have already mentioned you, or what companies have you worked with that are recognizable? Create a list of these moments and continue to leverage them and promote that you're associated with them.

To be an anomaly, learn to get comfortable praising your accolades. It's a tough pill to swallow, but there are ways to promote yourself without being cocky or blatantly promoting how awesome you are. If you're unwilling to share your wins with the world, it's a tough road to becoming an anomaly.

You have a series of events, accomplishments, and milestone moments in your life that have made you proud. These moments make you unique and special and are usually tied to an experience or big brand that the world knows.

Let's say you have been coaching football as an assistant coach for 26 years. That hard work finally pays off and you become the head coach. Now which sounds better on your resume: one year of head coaching experience or 26 years of coaching experience? Obviously that year of head coaching experience means a lot, however having over two decades of experience sounds a lot better. Additionally, if you have worked under anyone that has some clout, use their name as much as possible. Maybe you were coached under Hall of Fame Washington Redskins Coach Joe Gibbs. You can leverage the team's name and brand. Putting this all together, you have a 26-year coaching career and come from the Joe Gibbs coaching pedigree, which has three Super Bowl wins. Now you see how positioning your credibility into one that shows where you were groomed makes you look a heck of a lot more capable than a first-year head coach?

Maybe you have spent the last decade jumping from one job to another, and you're afraid that that will make your commitment to a new company questionable. There are ways to position yourself to make you look like a seasoned veteran, rather than someone with a short attention span. Leverage your school, especially if they have a big name or have big-name alumni. You graduated from an educational juggernaut which led you to a decade's worth of work with some of the top brands in hotel management like Hilton, Best Western, and MGM Grand. (Note: Never, ever lie on your resume because that is just setting you up for failure.)

In addition to your resume, look at the companies you have worked for. What big wins did they have that you had direct ties to? If you were in a department that won a credible award, don't you want to flaunt it and share its worth? Not everything ties directly to your past and that's okay. But if you have accolades showing how amazing you are, then you need to tell the world.

Let's say there's a female soccer player from the University of Southern California that was on the 2016 National Championship winning team but is now a doctor at Cleveland Clinic. Even though the championship win is long over, it would be foolish for her not to use that to her advantage in promoting herself from a business standpoint. She's an anomaly because she was a part of something that very few ever are. Even though she's now in a totally different field, she will always be a champion. Take a step back and look at your life as an outsider. *Tell your story! It's a good one.*

Lewis Howes, a popular podcaster, leveraged his professional career in football as a stepping stone when he first started in business. While his career was cut short due to a freak accident, he knew that he had unique life experience that would set him apart. Instead of forgetting his past, he used it to get in front of people with whom he wanted to be associated. A few years later, Howes is a best-selling author surrounded by some of the top businesses and brands in the world. He took his unique situation and turned it into an anomaly of a career. In addition to being a professional athlete, Howes can also promote himself as a best-selling author and popular podcaster with his podcast *The School of Greatness*.

It's all about credibility. When someone first "meets" a person, it's human nature to question them and ask why they should trust that person or care what they have to say. Your goal is to position yourself as someone who has credibility by leveraging your accolades, milestones, and endorsements. You do that and people will listen. You'll become an anomaly.

Once you overcome the fear of bringing yourself into the spotlight, it's time to do it over and over again. It's helpful to have a content calendar to keep your posts organized so you don't overshare one piece of content, or neglect another. A calendar can keep you on track and you can use a scheduler to automate your sharing.

-------------- **Roadmap** --------------

1. What big wins and milestones have you achieved over your lifespan?
2. What brands have you worked with?
3. What do you want people to think you do, or how can you help them? What keywords and phrases are associated with these?

Chapter 15

RINSE AND REPEAT

T hink about all the content you have produced. It's probably sitting in a photo library or on a web page and nothing is being done with it. That's okay, having content at all is the first step. Most people don't get started because they're afraid or they want their first post to be perfect. That "perfect" time never comes, so don't wait for it.

To reiterate, content is the material that you create for others to consume. It's often a blog post, an advertisement, a video, or a podcast interview.

If you're trying to start your career as a freelance photographer but haven't started an Instagram account because you don't think your work is good enough, stop thinking that way. Was Picasso's first painting amazing? Probably not. Do you think Aaron Rodgers threw a perfect spiral the first time he picked up a football? Maybe, but highly doubtful. Get over the idea that you're not good enough to show the world. You're not as good as you're going to be in the future, but that doesn't mean you shouldn't start now. The beauty of life is growth. And to grow you have to start.

In this section, we'll review what editorial and content calendars are and show you tools you can use to push out your content.

An editorial content calendar is when a media organization, like Barstool Sports, Bleacher Report, or BuzzFeed, maps out the different aspects needed for a story including interviews, editing, and writing, as well as when they're going to push out or release a story or article. A content calendar is a calendar of your content and when you're going to release each piece. It's important to merge these concepts together to take a look at what content you have plus when you want to continue to distribute.

You'll want to plan out your content for at least a month, if not a full year. The content you promote should be evergreen. **Evergreen content is content that stays true and relevant for a long time.** Create tags so you can see what content you already have, and fill in the holes where necessary.

You can create your calendar several ways—by purchasing a large calendar, by making one on a spreadsheet by opening up your digital calendar and scheduling out content release times, or by boxing out a grid on a blank sheet of paper. There are also a lot of programs that can schedule and manage your posts like Hootsuite, Buffer, and Meet Edgar. Map out the content you want to release. You can get creative and bulk certain content that pertains to a certain month or event and promote the content with a headline that you coin. Promote doesn't necessarily mean to purchase an advertisement, rather to promote or distribute the content that was created.

Content Calendar

Sun	Mon	Tue	Wed	Thur	Fri	Sat
Blog post	Press	Blog post	Review	Testimonial	Press	Review
Video	Blog post	Award	Video	Blog post	Award	Blog post
	News	Press	Blog post	Press	Video	
	Review	Testimonial	Podcast	Video		
		Video		Review		

Once you have an understanding of what content you already have and the new content you want to produce, you need to map it out on your calendar. Decide which dates and exact times you want to release content and on which platforms. A platform could be on social media, on your website, on another website, or even an email. The key is choosing a place and releasing it. In the beginning, don't set unrealistic dates or frequency for delivering new content. If it's hard for you to get one new piece of content out a week, don't expect to be able to do five in a week just because you have that on your calendar. It's unrealistic and will set you back, if not deter you altogether. The most important thing is to get yourself (and your team if you have one) into a publishing routine. If you do this, then you'll get your following into a routine to be ready for new content on the days and times you tell them to expect it, just like they would a favorite TV show. The sooner you begin to train them to expect something from you, the sooner they start telling their friends about you and sharing your content with them.

First We Feast produces viral content on its popular YouTube channel. Its most popular is a web series called *Hot Ones*, where host Sean Evans interviews celebrities and eats ten hot wings with them. With each wing the sauce gets spicier, as do the questions. (He asks questions not normally asked on a traditional interview show.) *Hot Ones* brilliantly sends out teaser videos through its social media on the days leading up to the show's weekly Thursday release. This does two things: It gets fans excited about the content, and it sets a weekly expectation on when the show is coming out so fans know to look for it. How many interviews for news segments have you watched in your life? All of them look the same, don't they? *First We Feast* turned the age-old interview into an anomaly. As the Complex front man, Sean Evans and his teammates came up with the idea to interview celebrities. They wanted the interviews to be anything but typical so they flipped the status-quo interview into a ten-wing eating questionnaire. With millions of subscribers,

> this new style of interview show has a lot of fans wanting
> more because it's unique and offers insights into the lives
> of celebrities you don't normally get with a typical interview.

Training your fans to tune into your content can also provide you a lane to promote new content. Popular business shows like *Entrepreneurs on Fire with John Lee Dumas* and *The Top* by Nathan Latka push new content daily, and they use this in their marketing messages. It makes sure they get daily visitors instead of just once-in-a-while visitors. You don't have to push content every day immediately, or, really, ever. Just know that as you grow it could be a strategy that can get more eyeballs on you.

Now that your content calendar is scheduled at the frequency you desire, you have to remember to release it. There are tools that allow you to upload your content to your preferred platform at the frequency you choose. If you're busy, lazy, or just plain forgetful, platforms like these are a godsend.

Meet Edgar, Buffer, and HootSuite are among the most popular platforms. These are reasonably priced from $0 to 50 a month. It may not seem worth it at first until you realize the time and energy they save you. Meet Edgar goes one step further than Buffer and HootSuite and recycles your content over and over again on a schedule you set up. With the other two platforms, you have to individually schedule each time you want to post content, even if it's the same content each time.

Be aware of the potential pitfalls of using tools like these. For example, Facebook's algorithm treats a video directly uploaded to Facebook more favorably than a YouTube link because it wants you to stay on its site as long as possible. They don't want people leaving to go to YouTube, one of its competitors. So, when using these tools, keep that in mind and make adjustments when necessary so you don't miss potential clients.

There's no exact science as to how much you should post, when to post, and on which platform. It's a skill that you develop along the way. If all you do is sell and ask your followers to buy, it's guaranteed that you won't do as well as if you spend more of your time educating, inquiring, and learning.

Having content already produced is great. But, you need to have a steady flow of new content coming out for several reasons. New posts on your website help you rank higher on search engines. And, keeping a constant flow of fresh, engaging content helps you keep your audience engaged. There's no limit on the type of content you can produce.

-------------- **Roadmap** --------------

1. Create a content calendar, or download a template at AnomalyMethod. com.
2. Determine what content you have, take an inventory, and fill out the AMR document with your content. What is the theme/type/topic?
3. Where do you want to share your content?
4. Create a schedule of when you want to post content (day and time) and through which channel or medium.
5. Which keywords, hashtags, and phrases will you use for your content?
6. Sign up for a social media scheduler and upload your content. Post the content on the times decided on in Step 4.

Chapter 16

DOCUMENTING

One of the biggest struggles people have is "What kind of content should I produce?" When starting out, a good way to come up with topics is to write down questions people have asked you about your business or what you do for a living.

On your website, you may have compiled a series of frequently asked questions. Promote these questions instead of hiding them on a page that doesn't get visited often. Keep a running list somewhere of questions that potential prospects or current clients ask. How can I get more followers? How do I make a Bundt cake? How do I turn my email list into more customers? What can I do to make a viral video? How do I find a job after college? How do I impress my boss to get a raise?

If you're still unsure of where to start, or need additional ideas of questions, poll your current social media following and email list. Ask them what questions they need answers to. Let's look at Amazon. They now produce pilot episodes for their content division. Instead of creating an entire series, they'll shoot a pilot and gauge interest from reviews, time watched, and engagement. This process allows Amazon to spend less time and money on content that may not produce returns. You can use this method as well by teasing out a piece of content before you even create it. If the engagement is lackluster, it shows a few possible outcomes: it's not what your targets are searching for; your content is not reaching your particular target customers; or you're simply not piquing their interest in the word choice or keywords that you used to describe the content.

Documenting describes the process of gathering information, so you can look back and reflect on your studies and conversations and use this information to improve. Documenting is also recording the conversations you have with prospects, clients, and others under a specific topic. To get started with documenting, start taking notes during the conversations that you're already having. Pull out your cellphone (or buy a $10 digital voice recorder from Amazon) and record the conversation. When you really feel comfortable, record via video and audio. This content doesn't have to be aired in any kind of manner. It's simply important to have documentation of what was said. How many times have you said something and thought "Wow, I wish I would have recorded that"? Documenting is that process.

Once you get in the habit of recording your conversations, or at the least taking notes, start analyzing and finding trends. Which questions are repeatedly asked and what types of reactions and keywords are created? Take notes on all of it. Over time, take the top questions and create content around them. However you choose to get the content out, the key is getting it from your head and into the world so others can find it, consume it, and be introduced to you.

In later chapters, you'll learn how to produce content that creates raving fans. But for now don't overcomplicate things. You're an expert in someone's eyes so take that knowledge, document it, and create what your targets are searching for. If you don't, guess what? Someone else will. You have the tools available to you so stop complaining about how your teammate or competitor is getting better results and go get them for yourself. Remember anomalies are focused. Talk to as many people as you can, as often as you can. The more conversations you have with your prospects, the more you'll understand what they're looking for and how you can help.

How many meetings have you attended where someone is picking your brain about something? You may not have realized it, but that's likely the craft or trade that you're good at. It's what others see you as an expert on or authority in. Instead of documenting the conversations you have for your own purposes, convince your guest that the conversation would be a wonderful addition to your content library, and then upload the conversation to the appropriate medium. This way you're not just having one conversation, you're having one conversation that can be seen by the world. Too often, you're wasting your time repeating yourself. It's one of the reasons *Anomaly* was written.

In 2013, I was speaking at an event on marketing and sparked the mind of a new business owner in the crowd looking to improve her site. Jess Horton, founder of The Fit Petite, asked me for help, so we met. I showed her a few tips that would help her improve her new website, including ways to make money from it. Afterward, I asked her to send me the notes as I had forgotten to record the conversation (yes, I am human, too). She astonished me at how many notes she took, but I knew if it was important enough for her to take pages of notes, these were questions other new business owners and bloggers had. I fired up my camera and shot a video documenting the conversation and Jess's questions.

Even the high school honor student who is asked for help in school by their classmates should start creating content on those topics. Jess Horton took the notes and acted on it, improving her site and finding new creative ways to monetize it. It was something she wanted to do but hadn't figured out how. The topics don't matter in the sense that what matters is that you recognize that you're a subject matter expert and need to get the content people are picking your brain about into the eyes of many more than a one-time coffee meeting.

One complaint to documenting or providing content around what you do for a living is this: "I don't want to share my secret sauce with the world. If I document or share this information, I'll be providing an inside look at how I make a living."

This technique is not about giving away all of your hard lessons learned or what sets you apart. Instead, think about the questions that you continually answer for new prospects. This book is an example of just that. I reflected on the questions that I was repeatedly asked. I concluded that it was some form of, "I have this great business, product, app, or opportunity to help others, but no one knows about it. How can I be seen?" *Anomaly* was born! I was already providing the answers in a plethora of different ways, just not in an all-encompassing book. I decided to change this.

> Erik Olson had a similar idea. He noticed that the calls and emails he would receive for his digital marketing agency, Array Digital, were mostly questions on "How much does it cost to build a website?" or "How much does digital marketing cost?" Array Digital decided to get in front of the matter and created content that shared the answers. They answer their frequently asked questions and make a big push so their prospects can learn what they need and in return create a relationship with Array Digital.

-------------- **Roadmap** --------------

1. What are the three most frequently asked questions people ask you?
2. Survey your following and ask questions on what troubles or challenges them or what type of content they are searching for.
3. Begin to record/document conversations. Do this by pen and paper, typing on a computer, or recording audio and video.
4. Review and analyze the conversations. Determine what the trend in conversations is and create content around that trend.

Chapter 17

THE 50-TEN CHALLENGE

Trust is important. People don't follow brands and personalities they don't trust. You're probably reading this book because you want to increase your exposure and want others to find you. To do that you need to gain their trust.

Imagine if you gain the trust of fifty new prospects. Now, let's say you could talk to those fifty new prospects for only ten minutes to better understand their wants and desires. (If you're someone looking for subscribers or fans, you can still use this same concept.) Find out what your prospects want. By asking questions, you can learn a lot. Providing a benefit to help someone move forward extends a huge amount of value for you. And, it helps you move closer to becoming trusted and an authority.

One of the biggest mistakes most people make is making something for the sake of making something. Maybe they think it's cool or entertaining, but no one else actually finds value in it. Think about the idea of the starving artist upset that no one is buying their art. They create and create, but never sell. This is because they're creating for themselves, and not creating what the market wants or needs. If you want to have a successful brand, you have to let the market guide you.

The 50-Ten Challenge is a series of lightning-fast meetings in a very short period of time, ideally less than three days. Yes, it's a lot of talking, but you provide value, have a lead, and show someone why they can trust you. Win, win, win! The 50-Ten Challenge is a series of 50 ten-minute conversations, via phone or Skype, or in person. The concept is to get in front of a lot of people really quickly to help identify their problems and needs. Think of yourself as a doctor. Listen to the way they describe what they feel, what they want, what their current issues are, etc. It's important that these conversations are one-on-one. Be sure to document and record them for your records. (Note: If you use audio and video, make sure to let the person know that you're recording. If they have a problem with it, go back to old-school note-taking and *don't* record without their permission!)

You should already have an understanding of your target customer. Now you need to find out where they spend their time, either online or in person. If your target market is dog owners, then there's a high likelihood you'll find most of your customers at vet's offices, dog parks, and pet stores. If your target customers are other business owners, networking events are great places to find them. Or maybe it's a social media marketer who could simply be at a coffee shop. All of these examples of target customers can also be found online in forums, groups, and webinars. If you're starting a new YouTube channel about soccer, then visit already established channels on the subject and look at the people leaving comments, liking the posts, and subscribing. This is a veritable gold mine for you!

Once you know who you want to talk to and where to find them, your next step is to collect their contact information. Sometimes it's right in front of you, and other times you have to dig. Either way, you can't make contact if you don't know how. If you have a mutual connection, ask for an introduction or their contact information. Communicate with your target directly. The majority of the time, messages sent to accounts like info@company.com are a waste of your efforts. Find the specific email address of the prospect you're trying to reach, like zack@startwithhatch.com. If it's too intimidating to start with someone you don't know or have never met in person, it's okay to start with some targets with which you already have some sort of relationship established.

The important thing is to reach out. If you're doing a social media post, it could be:

> Hey friends,
>
> I'm looking to learn what challenges you're currently facing in your businesses. I'd love to have a one-on-one phone call with you, free of charge, and just 10 minutes of your time would be phenomenal! I made it super easy for you to schedule by linking my calendar to when you're free. Please schedule your call today at (and provide a link to schedule).
>
> Thanks,
>
> Zack

This is short, sweet, and to the point. You're engaging with your following and letting them know you care and want to help them at no cost. If you make it easy by giving them a link, you'll have a better shot at getting people to sign up.

You can also do this as a post to an online forum or group, or to your group of followers through an email or social campaign. Be sure to follow the rules of the forum as not every group allows you to post and promote. Even though you're not actually promoting, some group leaders may see it that way. If they do, find another group that doesn't have those same requirements.

If you have an existing network, pair your network with your targets' qualities and see who fits the bill. Instead of posting on social media exclusively, send your target a message where you have had conversations in the past, or where you feel comfortable, and invite them to the conversation. Again, ease into this by starting with people you already know. Also, do this challenge in the mediums that you feel comfortable. If you hate meeting people in person, then try the phone or a video platform like Skype or Zoom. The more comfortable you are, the better your chances of completing this challenge.

Break down 50 call times at ten minutes each. You now have everything you need. One additional tool that may help you schedule is Calendly, which takes a snapshot of your calendar and shows your guests when you're available.

Stephen Reinstein created Market Muscles, an online services company that helps martial arts studios improve their online presence through websites, graphic design, and social media engagement. He built his company in early 2016, and a few months into developing the company he officially announced the business to the public. However, no one knew about him or cared, and, more importantly, no one knew what kind of value Market Muscles could provide martial arts studios.

For several months, Reinstein tried getting into the community with no results. That's when he used the 50-Ten Challenge. Reinstein found where his customers frequented, reached out directly through forums, and offered a free call to discuss the challenges that the studios were going through with their marketing and websites. These calls were really essential to him because the relationships that he made started to pay off. By providing value in a simple phone call, studios began to purchase his services.

When you're trying to get in front of someone but are challenged with the "how," stop doing what everyone else is doing and be the anomaly. Help your prospects and they'll, in return, help you. You know what everyone else is doing because you see it every day in your email inbox, in your mailbox, on your TV, and through your social media channels.

-------------- Roadmap --------------

1. Create a spreadsheet of targets for 50-Ten.
2. Sign up for Calendly.
3. Reach out to targets and ask for lightning discovery meetings.

Chapter 18

APPLY FOR AWARDS

Providing value to customers is what being a business is about, and if you're good at it, you can be labeled as the authority. One great way to do this is to apply for awards. There are millions of awards at the local, regional, national, and global levels. Winning awards not only labels you as an authority, but it provides you with free press and exposure. So don't be afraid to put your hat in the ring!

Winning is important for many people. Competitive or not, applying and nominating yourself or your business is an incredible way to be seen quickly in your community and niche. Millions of awards are given out each year in a number of areas.

Think about how many businesses want to be Inc. 5000 companies. Yes, it means you're ranking well against your peers, but even more than that, it gives you credibility. As you grow your business or brand into more of a powerhouse, you can use this technique to get that Inc. 5000 love even if it's just from your local newspaper.

To begin, find listings of awards and their nomination periods on a local and national level. You can search through publications you read or subscribe to and search their database to see if they have given out awards or "Best of's" in the past. If they have, then that trend will likely continue. They may be marketing for it currently. If they are, take a look at the qualifications needed. Your local newspaper or business magazine may do an annual "Best of" list. Track when they publicize and stay on top of this so when the time comes you're ready to rock. Most people don't apply or register for awards. For whatever reason they don't think that they're good enough or deserve to win. Stop thinking like this! If you qualify, apply!

As you apply for these awards you'll realize that many ask the same questions, so to save time create an ongoing document with your answers. Be sure to update the document with new accolades or when changes occur for you.

The possibility of winning will depend on the size of the brand giving away the award, with a Inc. 5000 company being the most difficult to win. Your local Chamber of Commerce "Best Business" might be a 5 out of 10 in difficulty and your local newspapers probably a 1 or 2 out of 10. Many of these awards and rankings are based on fan votes. If you have been doing a good job of creating a following, ask them for votes, and if your community is big enough their support alone should help you take home the prize.

If you lose, don't sweat it and, more importantly, don't let it stop you from applying for other awards. A lot of times the person who deserves it the most doesn't actually win. But, at minimum they at least get some free exposure and attention from the nomination. Keep applying to anything and everything you think you can win. Many people even promote that they were nominated for an award. How many times have you seen an artist advertised as a six-time Grammy

Award–nominated songwriter, or two-time Emmy award nominee? Even though they didn't win, it's impressive to see that they were nominated.

So, what if you win? Now it's time to market that you have won. Create a social media post around the win, a blog post thanking your following, and tag as many parties as possible in your content. On your website and marketing materials, add the logo of the award that you won. You may be thinking, "But I don't like to brag." This is not bragging. This is showing your credibility and that you're a boss in your industry.

Once you win an award for the first time, try to win that award for a second and third time. By saying and promoting that you're a three-time award winner of X award, it shows your audience that you're consistently considered one of the best.

If you're a photographer and won best image, when you post that image in the future, be sure to tag it and put in the description "award-winning photo in XYZ promotion." It promotes you as a champion. It gives a shout-out to the brand who gave you the award, which means they'll likely promote it to their networks over and over. This brings more exposure back to you.

Awards are winnable, and they're a credibility stamp. Try winning an award as early and as often as you can and in as many categories as you can. By doing so, you receive free mentions and press, increased exposure through social media, links to your work, credibility through the roof, and status as a boss in your industry or field. Awards can get you closer to your goals, even when you don't think you're qualified.

Tracy Link owns a security staffing business, Integrity Security Services, and was looking for ways to get exposure. She didn't have the budget of the big boys in her industry but was willing to do whatever she could to get that exposure. I told her to apply for awards as there are a lot of them out there to win. She immediately began looking for awards in the city where her business resided. To her surprise, she won. Winning this award, the Entrepreneurial Excellence Award, gave her a boost in confidence and now she had something to leverage. On all of her marketing materials, in all of her speeches, and on her proposals she mentions winning the Entrepreneurial Excellence Award. Winning an award may not be the deciding factor on whether or not someone will choose to do business with you, but it sure gives you a leg up in regard to credibility and expertise.

You can also apply to enter competitions. MadSkills creates virtual jobs for military spouses by connecting them to companies with teams distributed across the country. MadSkills is owned and operated by military spouses Erica McMannes and Liza Rodewald. When they were a new business, they were looking for creative and cost-effective ways to get awareness out about their business. MadSkills has entered a handful of competitions included SXSW, Patriot Boot Camp, Start Peninsula, and the Innovation Cup. Each of these events and the others that they participated in helped them in numerous positive ways, including cash prizes, growing their network, learning about a situation from someone who has already gone through it, or gaining exposure.

When I worked in television, I applied for a journalism award. Actually, I applied for dozens, and I ended up winning second place for one of them. Instead of being just journalist Zack Miller, I can now say I am award-winning journalist Zack Miller. Doesn't that make me sound a whole lot more credible? So, get out there, find out what awards you can apply for, and do it! What have you got to lose?

If you do win some awards, don't forget that as important as winning is to growing your brand, being humble and grateful is too. Going the extra mile to show your supporters how much they mean to you, and how much you appreciate their support, can do wonders for your brand. Like taking the time to do something personal, perhaps sending a handwritten card.

-------------- **Roadmap** --------------

1. Search for awards in your industry. Compile a list. If nominations are open and you believe you qualify, apply.
2. If you get nominated or win, add marketing around the nomination and win to your collateral. Share and distribute.
3. Create a text document to compile all similar application questions.
4. Add award-winning (or award name-nominated) to your title.

Chapter 19

HANDWRITTEN CARDS

When was the last time you met someone and got a "nice to meet you" handwritten card in the mail afterward? You probably can't remember, can you? A simple handwritten "thank you" or "pleasure to meet you" can do wonders for showing others you respect and appreciate them.

It has become the normal practice to begin a relationship with someone by exchanging email addresses and phone numbers and starting conversations that way. But, that's what everyone does. What does an anomaly do? They obtain the mailing address and send them a handwritten card. It could say anything like "nice to meet you," "I'm looking forward to a long and fruitful relationship," or something else very simple. Whether it's following up with someone you just met or sending a note to a guest you recently had on your podcast, the extra touch will be appreciated. Plus, it'll help you stay in their mind and that is exactly what an anomaly does. They stick in someone's mind and are rarely forgotten.

If you're applying to college or a job, the standard procedure is to send in a cover letter, or story about yourself, along with your resume, but you know that you're competing with dozens, possibly thousands, to get that acceptance (or job).

Paper and digital resumes all look the same. What can you do to be the anomaly? Don't just apply to the position. Learn who the acceptance committee is or the person handling the job interviews. Maybe it's the CEO or the HR person in the company. You can search who it is via their website or look to see where to send your application. Before you send in your required documents, you need to dazzle those making the decision about you before they even get your application or resume. Send them a handwritten card thanking them for the opportunity to review your application and let them know that you look forward to meeting them in person. People in these positions rarely receive anything that stands out like a handwritten note or card.

In TV news, hiring managers receive audition tapes of potential new team members. A reporter, anchor, director, editor, or producer looking for a new position puts together their "sizzle reel," a collection of their best work showing why they're a prime candidate for the position. The challenge is that every single sizzle reel looks the same. Sure, the content is different from person to person, but for the most part, every tape has the same feel to it. With hundreds of submissions for every new TV position available, the hiring managers spend hours looking through tapes, DVDs, or digital files until they finally find one they like. Most sizzle reels are viewed for just a few brief seconds, if at all. To be the anomaly, you must think creatively on how you can game the system or be seen by someone in a crowded world.

In addition to sending a handwritten card in advance of your application and/or resume, send food. In the newsroom, an applicant who really wanted a job would send a cookie cake with the stations call letters on it or a handful of pizzas. For just a few bucks, you're all but guaranteeing you'll be noticed and be given a more thorough look than the others. If you're applying to several jobs and money is tight, try to find similar ways that fit your budget to provide value or something unique to the hiring manager. If you're applying to 100 schools or jobs, it may not be advantageous to send a handwritten letter to each, and the additional costs for food, cake, or individualized items may be too expensive for you. Instead write the card and only pick a few locations to send something a little more special to. Your dream school or job, or top five, is a great way to start.

-------------- **Roadmap** --------------

1. Buy 50 simple cards (nothing fancy, blank cheap cards work).
2. Send a card to everyone you meet or want to be connected with. Rinse and repeat.

Chapter 20

THE RANKING OF WHO IS READY TO BUY

Understanding who your ideal prospect is and isn't can save you tons of time and money during your journey. Some people are ready to jump on board right away and some people need hand-holding. Knowing the difference is crucial.

Face it: Most people and businesses are not in the buying mode when you're battling for their attention. When you want them to buy, they would rather search Facebook and scroll through videos of crazy cats and adorable babies. It sucks. But, provide enough value and get them to engage with your content, and they'll get nosy and want more. Then and only then should you begin Step Five in the sales funnel.

We're surrounded by ads everywhere, but when is buying actually on our mind? Sure, we can be persuaded or conned into buying something we don't want, but that's not good business and should not be a practice that you live by. Getting someone's wallet out is difficult. Remember that stat from earlier in the book? Almost 68 percent of shopping carts are left with an item in it. It even happens to

Amazon. But, Amazon is smart. They built a program that sends emails to people who browsed items on their site and reminds them it's still available along with easy one-click purchasing.

Let's think about several locations of businesses or types of advertising and dissect whether people are in a prime buying mode or just being marketed toward. For the purpose of this example, let's rank each out of five stars, with five being very likely to buy right now and one star being very unlikely to buy right now. If someone is in a five-star buying mode, sell to them. However, if they're in a one-star buying mode, don't sell to them. Instead, learn more about them, provide value, and help them out where you can. Create a relationship. Plant the seed. A one-star can turn into a five-star, but that's up to you.

Who's ready to buy?

The first option is an easy one. Amazon, the world's leading ecommerce business. If you're on Amazon, you're looking to buy something. Your credit card information is already stored on the site, and you're only a few clicks away from buying what you need.

Amazon invented one-click purchasing so buyers don't have to pull out their wallets. You've probably noticed that many Internet browsers now capture your credit card information so all you have to do is select which one and your information is added to the transaction. It wouldn't be surprising if this was influenced by Amazon and other vendors requesting easier access to buyers' wallets.

The less you have to think about spending money, the more likely you're to buy even if money is tight.

Convenience stores like 7-Eleven and Wawa must have close to 100 percent closing rates. Think about it—when was the last time you saw someone walk in, look around, and NOT buy? It's not very often, and all these convenience stores need to do to sell is to be open and located where people are looking for them. Whether it's gas or a quick snack, convenience stores are a great five-star buying business mode. They play to people's needs of gas and food and they do it well. What can you do to be what people crave or need as much as a necessity like gas?

While shopping malls are popular places to shop, not every store is going to get business from every shopper. Window-shopping is the act of a potential buyer walking through and browsing a store's inventory. A shopping mall is a four-star for this reason. It's also a hangout spot for teens and young adults. Many malls are now creating experiences like free concerts, escape rooms, and amusement parks for cheap prices, with the hope that if you come for the experience you'll then walk around the mall and buy something. This is the same reason malls added movie theaters decades ago. Malls are typically anchored by a large big-box business, like Nordstrom or Macy's, and then filled in with smaller retail options in between. The anchor tenants tend to be the businesses that bring in the majority of mall shoppers. If you can get retail space in a mall, that is a great opportunity to introduce yourself to mall shoppers and share with them what makes your brand so special. You can take a one-star opportunity and turn it into a five-star in the same scenario.

If you're eating at a restaurant you're already a five-star, but how often are you upsold on an appetizer or dessert? These items are typically cheap to the vendor and cheap to the buyer. One study found that 50 percent of consumers order a dessert at dinner at least sometimes on a scale of always, often, sometimes, rarely, and never. This technique is used by several retailers—if you buy a device that needs batteries but don't have batteries in your cart, the retailer may ask you if you want batteries, and oftentimes those batteries are on a shelf at the checkout counter. RadioShack used to be the king of this. Panera Bread's online ordering system upsells you for items they notice you don't have in your cart when you go to check out. For instance, if you don't have a beverage, a pop-up fills your screen reminding you that you don't have one in your cart. If you have all of the normal items, they tempt you with a baked good for a slight discount. In store, if you forget a drink or are only getting a drink, they've made it easy to not even have to interact with a human. You go up, press a few buttons, swipe a card, and you fill up your own beverage; purchase is complete. Scary, but effective!

The top brands in the world have figured out little techniques to make their process easier. Looking at your business, why re-create the wheel when you can replicate what they're doing? They show you exactly what they're doing so why not take advantage of it and use it yourself with whatever budget you can? It's not stealing or copying. It's leveraging a process that works. Just document the processes you go through as a consumer and use them for your own purposes. You'll still need to work on your creative side of the process, but the playbook is the same.

Examples of three-star buying modes are a webinar, conference, or an email drip campaign. All three follow a similar methodology in that you find something people want to learn about or need solutions for and then provide them with ways to learn that information or get the solutions they need. Establish yourself as an authority, and then upsell them at the end when you have gained their trust. If a webinar is 60 minutes, then it's likely to be forty minutes of education, ten minutes of engagement and questions (or Q&A), and the remaining time shows a solution based on the education and Q&A. Same goes for a conference, except the time frame is longer. **An email drip campaign is typically a series of emails helping the reader learn a new trade and then an upsell of a solution that makes their problems go away.**

Instead of selling while your prospects are in lower buying modes, think of ways to encourage someone to learn more or follow your experience. YouTubers are notoriously good at this, or at least those with millions of subscribers. They provide amazing content, and at the end of their video, they ask you to subscribe. They know that if you subscribe you're asking for and want more, and they'll send you reminders to view their content. There are even tricks to add subscribe buttons in the video, so all a viewer has to do is click it and they're in. The easier you can make it for someone to subscribe, the better your chances are of getting subscriptions.

Networking events, as we discussed, are a great way to meet new people but they're not a great place to sell. Let me reiterate: As you attend these events, be sure to listen more and follow up later.

Direct mail is a multibillion-dollar industry. If mastered, it can be highly lucrative, but there has to be a reason for the business or consumer receiving the mail to get excited—like receiving coupons or discounts.

> Pool Scouts, a growing franchise business who provide pool cleaning and maintenance services, has found that target prospects become customers if they send direct mail. It takes up to six mailings for them to convert, but it works. They offer first-time incentives and well-designed postcards to only those they deem their targets. Since they have franchises all across the United States, they have to be cognizant of what a different area is looking for. People in Wisconsin close their pool for the winter, while people in Florida may never close theirs.

Unless someone is really selling to a pain point that a consumer is currently going through, these one-star buying modes should be used to get people in the door and then taken through the sales funnel. A cold call, random office visit, outdoor billboard, and a meeting without an agenda are all going to be one-star buying modes. Again, it's important to know what buying mode a prospect is in, and if they're not in a five-star mode, your goal is to introduce yourself or your brand to them and share something unique about you and/or incentivize someone to learn more about you. Restaurants do this by offering a free appetizer for a first-time guest, gyms offer one-week free trials, and some online business offer thirty-day free trials. The idea is to let the viewer know you're open for business and that you want them to be a part of yours.

An outdoor billboard, while being seen by many eyeballs daily, isn't always the best way to advertise. When you're driving you have to see the advertisement, consume it, analyze it, and memorize it, all within six seconds since that's about the amount of time you have before you have passed it. So, for your business, what can you do to make a quick impact on your target customers? Think outside the box!

The next time you're at a retail store or shopping online, look at the techniques they use to get people to make a purchase and implement these strategies into your brand. Whether you're selling something or not, these techniques can help you go from zero to hero.

-------------- **Roadmap** --------------

1. Dissect what buying level your targets are in 1 to 5.
2. Create a plan to get them to level 5.
3. Devise a strategy to "Just say, hey" to introduce yourself to new targets.
4. Are there add-ons in your arsenal that you can provide at checkout?
5. What content do you have that is popular?
6. Document your current checkout system, find the holes or opportunities, and tweak (for inspiration, review the stores and online where you purchase).
7. What pain point are your targets looking to be addressed?

Chapter 21

REPEATABLE
SEARCHABLE CONTENT

S ince the mid-2000s, social media platforms have been adopted by every generation and are built into almost every brand's awareness strategy. Even smartphones are built with social media platforms in mind as these phone companies and their carriers want their users to spend as much time as possible on these devices. Creators of content, websites, and social media campaigns often-times don't understand how these social networks function even if they build large, relevant brands on them. And you're often creating a brand solely assuming that the technique that works today will still work in the future. Or, even worse, betting that social media outlets will continue to encourage your visitors to come back over and over without you having to do anything. Yes, with billions of people on social media, it's a great tool to use to grow your business and for your brand to be seen, but you're playing in their sandbox—and they know it.

Some of your best campaigns and posts may never be seen just a few days after they're posted for the first time. Your posts are quickly buried by the heaps of content from everyone else. Because of the way sites like Facebook, Twitter, and

LinkedIn were developed, the content needs to be fresh and updated constantly. Social media sites don't index the same way that a website or blog post would. Websites need to be indexed, meaning the Internet or search engines understand what's being produced on those sites. A search engine scrapes the information that you provide in your posts and ranks the keywords associated against other similar posts.

An algorithm developed by the social media site is what determines which links and pages show up when you do a search. The caveat is that everyone is on social media and you don't want to lose out on the opportunity to have billions of eyeballs today, but you also want your content to be found tomorrow and beyond.

Creating repeatable, searchable content allows you to still create your following through social media, but builds the content that provides you with maximum results in the future on a website that you own. Now that you understand why your content is not being found on your social media platforms, what can you do to fix this problem? The simple answer is leverage social media to get views. But you also need to create similar content on mediums that you own, like a website, or physical collateral like business cards, brochures, mailers, etc.

Social media platforms own your content; you own the content on your website. If you put all of your content on social media and they change their strategy for how it's distributed, you could end up losing big time. Again, each platform is designed differently, and they don't love posts with external links or articles that take viewers from their sites. Why would they? They want the eyeballs so they can get their ad revenue. Build up your social followings and add a call-to-action link in a smaller percentage of your posts, or if you do video or images, give the URL you want visitors to go to. An image can have the text URL. If all your posts contain links to your work, the social media platform's algorithms won't give you as much love as they would if you were using the platform the way they want you to. Heck, Instagram only allows you to provide one link and it's in your bio. They want you to only post images and videos with a description and hashtags. They make it difficult to get off their site. This is where having a maximized profile is crucial.

Let's take a video you record on YouTube, Facebook, or LinkedIn. It gets a lot of love and you want to make sure people can find it later. Now, if a visitor is scrolling forever on your page they would be able to find it. Make it easy on them by giving the content a compelling headline and posting it to your blog. Use the full video and embed it along with a story. Add keywords so a visitor can search for this content and they'll be directed to a site that you control, and it'll be more convenient for them since they won't have to go hunting it down. If you use the right keywords and headlines, it should be fairly easy for them to find in a search.

Once they're on your site, make sure you have call to actions that will encourage them to get to Step 2 of the sales funnel, where they provide you with contact information of some kind. You can add this link via an image or hyperlinked text at the bottom of your post. The longer a visitor stays on your site, the better your chances of them becoming a customer. And if you have your funnel set, this can be streamlined.

There are tools that can make this easier for you. But, again, social media doesn't automatically do this. Whether you produce a video or image, you need to tell the search engines what they're looking at. You do this by telling the story in your blog posts and linking the images index. Roughly 25 percent of websites are built on WordPress. WordPress is a content management system and has become an easy-to-use tool to get your content laid out and make it understandable to search engines.

When you upload an image, the WordPress site will automatically ask you for a title, caption, alt text, and a description. These are all opportunities for your image to tell what it is to a search engine. It is best practice to use different phrases for each of these entries. So, if the image is the cover of this book, the title could be: *Anomaly: How to Finally Stand Out from the Crowd* book cover. The caption could read, "This is the book cover from the soon-to-be bestseller by Zack Miller, *Anomaly*." The alt text could be a series of keywords associated with the book that are not on the title or caption. For *Anomaly* those would be:

"What would you do to stand out from the crowd?"

"How can you get someone to look up from their laptop?"

"You have to be the anomaly."

And, finally, the description could be "*Anomaly* provides proven financially conscious and easy-to-implement methods for those who want to turn heads, be memorable, and become the anomaly! Rather than rambling about high-level topics that turn out to be nothing more than a plethora of cliché 'rah-rah' phrases that are supposed to get people excited about business, award-winning businessman Zack Miller shows readers what they can do *today* to grow their brand."

Building a social media pantheon can be huge in your journey to becoming an anomaly, but remember that social media is an "always relevant" tool and if you want your content and brand to be seen over and over years into the future, create content that can be indexed and searched in search engines.

-------------- **Roadmap** --------------

1. If you have not yet, buy a website. (Your first one at GoDaddy is only a buck. Buy it now.)
2. Sign up for a WordPress account.
3. Insert your content into the site.
4. Download a plugin called Yoast SEO, activate it, and get your content to a green-light stage.

Chapter 22

HOW TO STAND OUT

I f you want to stand out, you can't be like everyone else. That's being the anomaly. Think about a networking event that you go to and everyone looks the same. How can someone be different at a place where every single person is the same?

Let's review some of the biggest brands and how they're an anomaly.

Amazon is the leading ecommerce business in the world. One crucial feature to helping Amazon attain this status is the frequency in which a customer can receive a shipment. When a customer thinks about buying something on Amazon, they think, "Should I buy this on Amazon, or should I go drive to a different location and waste my time?" These customers have been trained to understand that if something isn't urgent, they can receive their package within a day or two. Amazon has gone even further to create two-hour delivery in many cities. Why would someone ever need to go to a store again with a service like that? Amazon is one of the major reasons why big-box stores have closed, and it's because they've made it über convenient for others to get their packages and not have to lug them around.

Zappos, which was purchased by Amazon, got its claim to fame by providing amazing customer service. Zappos sold shoes online. Nothing too crazy, but their wild culture and customer service got customers to give them a double take. When Zappos delivered a package, customers would open up their package containing their purchase and find a handwritten card, extra socks, or an item they were not expecting. Going that extra step can take a current customer and turn them into a raving fan. And that is exactly what Zappos has done. When hiring, Zappos offered their new employees cash to leave the business if they felt that Zappos wasn't for them. Zappos cares about their employees and their customers and understands that if both parties are super pumped about Zappos, their brand grows. Zappos CEO Tony Hsieh said that, "Zappos is a customer service business that sells shoes."

How about Chick-fil-A? When you step into one of their stores, or drive through their drive-through, you're getting a similar process to other fast food restaurants. But, when you get to the register, you can immediately tell that you're being treated with respect and care. When you dine at other fast food spots, what are the words that you associate with that establishment? Oftentimes those words are not very positive, but more times than not your experience at Chick-fil-A is one that is positive and makes you want to come back. Chick-fil-A has mastered customer service and goes even further to show guests what a pleasure it is to serve them. When a guest says thank you, a team member of Chick-fil-A says, "My pleasure." These two simple words help Chick-fil-A show off their customer service skills and make the customer want to come back, even if they had to wait in a line for thirty minutes.

Planet Fitness, a 24/7 gym hyped up to be the "non-bro" gym, boasts not having weightlifters throwing around weights and grunting. They even have a sign that says, "No Grunting." Planet Fitness discovered their target customers don't like to go to other gyms because they feel embarrassed or ashamed that they don't measure up to the physiques of the members of the other gyms. Planet Fitness thus created an environment that is welcoming and different from other gyms on all fronts, even going as far as to have a bold color scheme and "bad food" day. Planet Fitness wants those who feel left out and uncomfortable at other gyms to walk in and feel great about their experience. Planet Fitness' unconventional stance makes it an anomaly while positioning the rest of the fitness world as fairly standard.

In the 1980s, Vince McMahon Jr. took over his father's business, World Wrestling Entertainment (formerly WWWF and WWF). Wrestling in its existence was broken into territories—a series of small promotions tied to a geographical area. WWE owned a territory in the Northeast corridor of the United States. McMahon was ready to spice this up and acquire territories and build one mega-brand which is what people know as WWE today. McMahon took a huge risk. His biggest, according to him, was creating WrestleMania in 1985, the Super Bowl of wrestling. At WrestleMania, his wrestlers met with celebrities to put on the show of shows once a year. McMahon saw more in wrestling and knew he could build a worldwide brand from it. Today, it's a multibillion-dollar business with WWE being the brand with more social media followers than any other sports brand. McMahon's risk not only paid off in huge dividends, but branded him as a pioneer, or, as I like to put, an anomaly.

McMahon was also great at creating brands around his characters, specifically Dwayne "The Rock" Johnson. Johnson played on a National Championship team at the University of Miami and wanted to be a professional football player, but it never came to fruition. Instead, with a couple bucks to his name, he turned to wrestling and cemented his legacy on the Mt. Rushmore of Wrestling with his catchphrases, eyebrow raising, and blazing microphone skills. The Rock became the anomaly in the WWE. Fans couldn't resist his voice. Johnson, who has lightly retired from wrestling and moved to Hollywood, is one of the highest-paid actors in the business with his movies grossing over $1 billion. The Rock realized that his WWE character could become larger than life and by setting himself apart from the rest of his wrestling mates, he stood out and became a fan favorite—and his persona was even the bad guy!

These brands and personalities are all different than their industry peers. They created raving fans who constantly push their content to their networks and friends. By not doing what everyone else does, you'll stand out and not be lost in the crowd.

After a 12-year career as an airman in the Air Force, Tim Ryan decided it was time to retire from the military. Ryan wanted to become a businessman and, after a short stint in consulting with Booz Allen Hamilton, he took his talents and started his own business, Arcphor. Arcphor is a boutique business agency which consults with businesses to help them improve their web and digital presence through websites, social media, training, business planning, and grant writing.

However, even after a storied career in the Air Force, Tim was a nobody in the business community. He needed to find a way to be different, to stand out—and, of course, to be the anomaly. So what did Tim do? He decided that instead of reaching out to people saying "Buy my thing," he would reach out to them and create a relationship and offer them the opportunity to make money for any introduction that was sent his way.

Knowing that his brand and business were in its infancy, he understood that if he could leverage someone else's brand to promote his, he would have a better opportunity to make that relationship worthwhile and grow his business at the same time. So, he created a list of influencers that he thought would be a great fit to connect with and did a cold outreach via email which said:

"Hey, I'm Tim Ryan and I'm new to business after my career in the Air Force. I started a business called Arcphor. Ultimately I'm just trying to grow my relationships and I would love to meet with you and learn about your business."

If Ryan felt the conversation was going well with any given connection, he would offer an affiliate package to them. During these conversations he would say, "If you share or introduce me to anyone and we land that business, I would love to give you a piece of the business that was secured."

> Instead of just saying "Buy my thing," he said, "Let's work together," which made him and his business become an anomaly. At the end of every new meeting, Ryan would ask his guest if there's someone else he should contact, which allowed him to leverage their name to create a new relationship.

Ryan Williams is the author of *The Influencer Economy* and the host of *Stories of The Influencer Economy* podcast. Williams is a storyteller and has a very unique way of helping businesses, brands, and personalities stand out and be the anomaly. Through interviewing over 100 guests on his show, he started to recognize a trend: Most of the world isn't telling their own story. Instead, they let others tell it for them, which often leads to their story being butchered, incomplete, and the reason why their goals were not achieved. You know your story because you lived it, and it needs to be told by you.

While Williams was working for several large brands that had been acquired by Disney and Warner Bros., he discovered they're repeatedly telling the same three stories. That these three stories should always be in your back pocket: the underdog story, the badass authority story, and your fixer story. The underdog story is similar to a TED Talk, where you're trying to show that you have been in a rough spot in life, or in the shoes of your listeners. Think of the movie *Rudy,* where an undersized college student walks on to Notre Dame's football team. The underdog story is when you're an outsider and become an insider. In David and Goliath, you're an underdog and win. The badass story is sharing that you are amazing at what you do and the fixer story is showing how you solve a problem.

Why these three stories? They're an opportunity for you to really home in on a story that you know well instead of trying to come up with new content every single time. By trying to come up with a new story or angle for each and every time you are interviewed, it can be tough. By, instead, homing in on your three stories, you become more confident in your vocal release and others will begin to share the stories as you want them to over and over to help you build clout around those three stories in your back pocket. It makes sense if you think about it. Most famous people, celebrities, and A-listers tell the same stories over and over because they're getting in front of a different audience every single time. So instead of trying to create new content for every single episode, Williams believes you should have these three in your back pocket.

Part Three of *Anomaly* gives you specific techniques to use different platforms to get more eyeballs on you and your business. These methods and techniques detailed in the following pages have been proven time and time again.

-------------- **Roadmap** --------------

1. What can you do to be unique?
2. What are your three stories—a.k.a. your underdog, authority, and fixer story?

PART 3

ANOMALIES IN THE WILD

Chapter 23

INTRODUCTION TO THE ANOMALY

T o be an anomaly, you have to think differently, act differently, and stand out from everyone around you. Over the coming chapters, it's imperative to understand the concept of taking control of your content, marketing, and communication. For example, if you're on someone's podcast, they'll promote it once it goes live, and maybe sometime in the future. Let's say you were interviewed on a podcast and were on fire, spitting out knowledge bombs of wisdom, and know the message you conveyed was one that you want others to hear. Are you going to wait for *Joe's Podcast* to promote your episode again, or are you going to promote it on your end?

Most strategies don't work on their first try. If you execute a campaign and it bombs, learn why it bombed and why you didn't get the engagement you wanted. It doesn't mean that it was wrong or was the wrong target; there are always a few ways to do the same technique. Keep trying different concepts until one sticks.

In the coming chapters you'll learn examples of how to take already existing and new content and turning it into a recycle machine that will give you the results you were hoping for when it was first created.

Chapter 24

MAXIMIZING YOUR SOCIAL PROFILES

While social media platforms change, you can easily create a rock-star profile that helps you boost your brand. To maximize each of your social media platforms, you must first understand what each platform wants. While each platform is different in some regards, most, if not all of them, have options to upload a profile image and/or cover photo, write a description, and offer a place to provide links to other accounts or websites. This is your chance to stand out by maximizing your profile so that when people peruse your page, you're showing them the incredible human you are.

A maximized profile is essential if you want to be an anomaly. For starters, your profile must make it easy for a visitor to understand who you are and how you can help them. This also keeps you from coming across as that pushy cable salesman, rather, your profile does the talking for you.

Let's begin with profile pictures. Whether you're promoting a brand or a personality, your profile picture is typically a headshot of you or a logo of the business. But, just because everyone else does that doesn't mean you should. So why

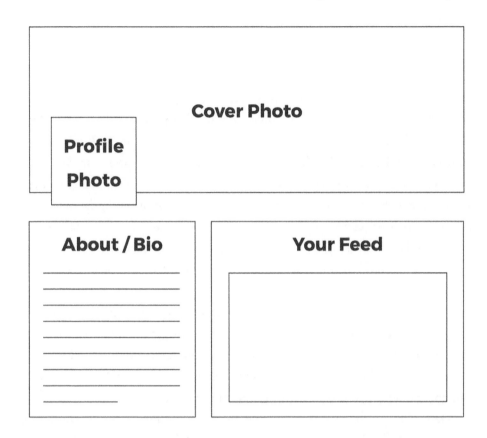

not throw some flair and personality into your profile pic and make it more fun. If you look like everyone else, there's little chance people will give your profile a second look. You don't have to go all out, just think of ways to be creative. Instead of a standard professional headshot, think about a caricature of you or one of you in action, like running or skydiving. There are no rules from the social media platform, so go for it. Show off who you are. If you own a pet, think about taking a picture with the pet. People love seeing pictures of cute pets!

Many social media platforms have a cover photo where you have more space to showcase who you are. Use this space to share a photo that demonstrates your "big wins" or something unique to you and/or your business. It could be just one picture or a collage of images that may include logos, brands, or awards.

Let's say you're a business that supports Habitat for Humanity. You can create a cover photo showing the team building a house and then some key stats or accolades, like how many homes were built this year, or the amount of money raised. You can also add contact information as a call to action to learn more or how to become a donor or volunteer. You have the space and people are looking at the picture, so be sure to provide them with a way to get in touch. On Facebook, specifically, with images you're also provided the ability to add text and a link in the description. Use this space to give a quick idea of what people are looking at along with a link. Again, you have free space to showcase yourself, use it. If you leave it blank, you're missing a valuable opportunity to catch peoples' attention!

If you don't have a designer to help you with these custom images, you can use sites like Fiverr or Canva. Fiverr is a marketplace that offers digital marketing solutions that start at $5, including design services. Canva is an online site that offers templates and designs for those without in-house services. Canva allows you to drag and drop images and add text to them so you can bring boring images to life.

Each social media platform allows you to tell your story in a unique way, whether it's 280 characters on Twitter or through images on Instagram. And it's *how* you tell that story that really matters. With any description you provide it's a short snippet of who you are. Keywords are important to include along with something unique about you that you want the world to know.

Depending on the platform, you may include your links in the description or you can add them where they ask for links. Be careful though, you can quickly write too much copy, and you don't want the TL;DR (Too Long; Didn't Read) effect. Tell the story you want your followers to know about you. Take the keywords and big wins from previous experiences in your life and frame your story around it. You could also showcase one of your three stories from your back pocket (remember Ryan Williams earlier in Part Two?). If you do a poor job of telling your story, people won't understand who you are and how you can help them.

Position yourself as the credible expert and you'll turn heads and create a following with your target customers. Don't be concerned if someone who is not your target audience doesn't like your profile and feeds. They're not your targets and can distort your thoughts. Heck, they can even be cancerous, so disregard them!

A good way to get people onto your profiles is to get content produced about you. Whether locally, nationally, or globally, produced content can be a great way to drive traffic to your profiles and website. A lot of people doubt their work and do not think they are strong enough or "press worthy." They think receiving a produced piece of content or press is hard to get or that they're not unique enough to be written about. That's just not true. Anyone can get press if they follow a simple series of steps.

-------------- **Roadmap** --------------

1. Take keywords from Chapter 14, Question 3 to use in the messaging of your maximized profile.
2. Snap or upload a fun image of you as your profile picture—don't be lame, have fun! I promise this will provide way better results than you think.
3. Create a more in-depth cover photo telling who you are and upload.
4. Sign up for Canva if you do not have access to in-house graphic design.

Chapter 25

WHAT TO DO WHEN YOU GET PRESS

Have you ever wondered how the media gets a news story or decides which stories to run or write about? If a story is "breaking news," such as an accident or fire, in your local town, a newsroom likely heard about it from a viewer who is seeing it firsthand, or they listen to police scanners and then send a crew to the scene.

A newsroom is the collection of all of the working parts of a news organization, which includes reporters, journalists, anchors, writers, producers, directors, photographers, editors, managers, IT, and many others who work collectively to get a series of stories out to their targets. You likely will never be a breaking news story, but it's important to know what you're up against and how these organizations work.

Media can be defined as your standard press like NBC, Fox, CBS, ABC, or modern media like BuzzFeed, Tasty, or Inc. The former report the news, while the latter produces soft or non-breaking news content, but both are considered press.

For softer stories that are not as hard or breaking, it's typically discovered through a relationship or referral from a reporter. In many cases, reporters are set to a "beat," which is a singular focus like a specific industry, business, crime, etc. These reporters exclusively produce content around their beat instead of randomly selected stories.

Stories are pitched to newsrooms day in and day out. Imagine it similar to a cold call you receive. Newsrooms are about as excited for cold-call story pitches as you are about receiving a telemarketer call during dinner. If you annoy someone and ask for something without providing anything in return, what do you think is going to happen? If your pitch was in a tangible form like on a piece of paper, it would get balled up and used as an office basketball for a game of trash-can ball.

Instead, think about an approach that creates a relationship with a reporter on the beat that makes the most sense to your industry. Open up a spreadsheet and start collecting information on reporters who could possibly do a story on you. Yes, you're creating these friendships with the hopes that it can turn into something for you, but if you create a genuine relationship with the reporter, you'll find that you can both provide value to each other. You can find these reporters by reading stories in your local, national, and world mediums with similarities to what you do and then look for who created the content. Collect their name, organization, email, phone number, and social media handles and put them in your spreadsheet. It may also be advantageous to collect where you found them, the story they wrote, and any other details that you can use in your future conversations. Reporters do move from organization to organization so be sure to update your spreadsheet every few months.

Once you have their contact information, reach out and introduce yourself. You can do this by email or social media. It's not recommended to do this by phone call. If by social media, think about liking or commenting on a recent post by the reporter and sharing your feedback. Reporters love positive feedback. Here's a little secret—reporters have egos, so if you stroke their egos, guess what? They'll like you more! A bonus would be to provide them more details on their article, which allows them to make their story better.

If reaching out by email, make it simple.

Hey Anna,

I just read your story about marketing in Boston. I really enjoyed it and have bookmarked your work, so I can stay up to date in the future. Did you know about this new way to produce a Facebook Live post? It's awesome. Have a wonderful day.

Best,

Zack

Let's dissect this email. First, you're reaching out to someone. Most people are too afraid to do that. Second, you prove that you read her article by specifically mentioning it, which makes her feel good, then you stroked her ego even more by saying you want to see more from her. Finally, you provided value by showing her something she may not know. This could be the first real opportunity for her to look at you as a source.

Ultimately, your goal is to become a source for the reporter. Instead of getting one article produced about you, the goal is to get dozens or hundreds of snippets and having reporters call you when they have questions. Or becoming the authority in your industry, even if you're new.

Don't become a stalker though. Judge each of these new connections with some self-control. If they write four stories a day, please don't email them about every publication. Instead think about giving a shout every few weeks. This takes practice to really gauge the correct timing, but you'll figure it out from their response back.

Have you noticed that you have not pitched anything about your business yet? That's intentional. The idea is to never pitch your business until you know you have a proven two-way relationship with the reporter. Everyone sends in press releases and prays they're seen, or emails a reporter saying they're the best thing since sliced bread. Even if you're the next best thing, this method doesn't work, so don't try it.

-------------- **Roadmap** --------------

1. Determine your target keywords and beats.
2. Create a spreadsheet or download at AnomalyMethod.com.

3. Search for media members creating content around your keywords and their beats and add their information to the spreadsheet.

4. Introduce yourself to them. ("Just say, hey.")

Chapter 26

RELATIONSHIPS ARE CRITICAL IN THE GROWTH OF A BUSINESS

Yes, the send and pray method works occasionally, but building a relationship pays far better dividends over the long term. You want a reporter to think about you as a source, and you want them to pitch your business. This method helps me get hundreds of stories produced about my company and companies that I consult or mentor.

Relationships are critical in the growth of a business. If you don't have any relationships, how do you expect to have sales and growth? You can't. There's no way to track how quickly this method can work for you to get sales or exposure, but people typically trust media organizations. To be able to leverage their credibility is a tremendous opportunity for whatever you're working on. And maybe the best thing about having these relationships is that reporters have other friends in the same market—and globally. Imagine the introductions they can make for you after you continue to help them! Endless.

If you have never had an article written about you or your business, start with a smaller publication. Begin with your local media, learn the process, and then move on to national or global media once you have a better understanding of expectations. They aren't that different, but you may get nervous trying to talk to Tom Brokaw instead of your local 23-year-old fresh-out-of-college reporter, or a writer at BuzzFeed.

It's a reporter's job to be nosy. If you have your social media profiles maximized and you create a relationship, they'll peruse your profile to learn about you before you even need to make a pitch to them. Or, even better, have a link to your business or piece of content in the footer of your email. Reporters are paid to investigate and gather information. If they're going to investigate you, give them some great information and interesting social media pages to peruse!

Several media outlets have free ways for you to quickly get exposure. If you live in an area with a newspaper or online media company, they're likely looking for content and promote free opportunities to do so, whether it be a quick promotion, new hire, upcoming events, promotions, or even business wins. Business wins could be things like landing a new big client, hiring employees, expansion, etc. These media companies are hungry to fill space with content and it's an easy way to get mentioned.

You can search a media organization's site, or email their newsroom, to find free opportunities to share updates on your business. Don't mistake this as submitting a news story. You're looking specifically for sections that talk about business wins, new hires, expansion, and the like. This is different than an advertisement. Not every outlet offers these opportunities, but if they do, take advantage of them.

HARO, which stands for Help a Reporter Out, is a free online tool connecting sources to reporters who are typically on a short deadline and are looking for experts to provide interviews. No relationship is needed here. A media organization needs content and you want exposure. HARO pairs the two together.

To get access, visit HARO and provide common signup information and select the type of information you can provide. You'll receive emails with a series of requests from reporters. Some HARO reporters could be looking for an expert on topics such as time management or goal setting. Others want sources for starting a business or for best social media tips. Dozens of examples are sent daily from HARO. Once you discover a request that fits you or your brand, follow their instructions and provide your feedback. Sometimes you're pitching to get an interview and sometimes they take your answers and run with it.

Keep in mind that submitting an inquiry doesn't mean that you'll get an opportunity for exposure, but this does increase your chances. Imagine being featured on *Fox News* because you provided a comment through HARO—for free. The opportunities that you can leverage from that could be monumental. Remember, you're trying to become or increase your authority status, and this is a great way to help you. HARO works with media organizations like *Reuters, Time,* the *Chicago Tribune,* and many more. You can learn a lot from HARO, and if you get a reporter's attention, it can create a long and ongoing relationship. Tip for HARO: If you keep getting passed on or receive zero callbacks, adjust your copy, or information you send, until you start getting contacted. Keep copies of what you send so you can improve upon it. Send your message to a few friends or colleagues to see what they believe could be adjusted, tweaked, or redone. You don't have to be an expert in copywriting, but a well-packaged message, the right keywords, and the best answers to the reporter's questions gives you the best chances at getting exposure.

The word "expert" may scare you. Don't let it. Instead, think of yourself as an expert in your industry, which makes you more qualified to the reporter who is looking for help.

Flypdeck is an electronic handheld game—think Bop It meets a fidget spinner meets a skateboard trick. The founders of the company, John Fuller and Bryce Wells, were looking for ways to get exposure and did not know where to start. As a young business, they understood that if they could leverage the branding of a media outlet they could get thousands of eyeballs on their product.

They learned that their local media outlet had a submission for "Startup Spotlight," which is similar to the opportunity detailed above, when media organizations look for companies to feature. They submitted Flypdeck to the outlet and were picked up within days. Before this opportunity, they had zero mentions outside of friends and family. After they were picked up, people learned about them and they were picked up again and brought onto a local radio show, received several speaking opportunities to present their business, and were even asked to be on a few podcasts. All of this occurred just by submitting their business to an outlet looking for story ideas. Flypdeck went a step further and reached out to several popular YouTube channels to see if they would feature or review their toy. They were shocked by the yeses they received. They sent a package of their games to these channels, along with a handwritten note and instructions. Their game is now being played, reviewed, and showcased on channels that have millions of subscribers and visitors. Talk about gaining some exposure!

Kenya Williams owns an auto-detailing business called iShine. He quit his cushy six-figure career working for a government contractor and instead took his skill set and love for cars and built a business. He was new to business and new to promoting himself, but Williams was looking for ways to gain exposure and had no idea where to start. Just like the team at Flypdeck, he found an opportunity for a local outlet to pick him up and within days he now had press about his business. Williams, now in his third year of business, is able to leverage and position himself as more of an authority since he's had media outlets produce content about—and promote—his business.

Positioning is one of the most important things in becoming an anomaly. It's not only understanding what you have done, but how and why people will look at you differently when they see you as a credible source. You're trying to convince someone that you're an authority, you're credible, and that you can help them or provide value to them.

Danny Rubin is a former journalist turned author. He took the period of his life and his skills that he learned from the University of Virginia and University of Maryland, along with a career in television news, and positioned himself as an authority. The word "author" is a derivative of the word "authority." Rubin is the author of *Wait, How Do I Write This Email?* and *Wait, How Do I Promote My Business?* Both books combine his decades of experience as a journalist and helping businesses gain exposure.

After many years, Rubin had grown sick of the rat race in TV news and wanted something different. He knew that he had the ability to do it. So where did he start? As an author he decided to put pen to paper and started a blog. At the time it was called *News To Live By.* Rubin didn't stop to think about all that he might lack, but instead put one foot in front of the other and made something happen. This is a key principle of this book. If you continue to wait and wonder, others will take your thunder and your audience, and you'll never find the success you so deeply desire.

He then turned his blog posts into longer-form ebooks and one of these ebooks, *25 Things Every Young Professional Should Know by Age 25,* got picked up by *HuffPost.* When you have a maximized profile, and you have content that is being shared by hundreds or thousands of people, big brands start to see it and share it. This means more people who consume those larger brands begin to see it. Rubin understood that if he could leverage the keywords and pain points that we've been talking about in this book and then get his work featured in big publications, he could then promote and position himself throughout his material. When people come to your site or people learn about you from a trusted entity, they don't question if you're someone who can help them. In Rubin's example, "As Seen On *HuffPost*" helped build his credibility stamp.

Even in the digital world, people still believe that being an author of a book is one of the biggest accomplishments you can make. And when you have testimonials galore from your work, you combine all of these things together.

Rubin loves helping others become better at their jobs and at their businesses and he had the skill set for it. So, he wrote a book about his expertise. His first book, *Wait, How Do I Write This Email?,* details how to write emails to certain people when you don't have a clue as to how. As a writing authority, he got asked the same questions over and over again: How do I follow up with a job interview? What can I say to clients who might be on the fence? Instead of answering the same questions a thousand different times, he put them into a book complete with email templates and thorough explanations. Rubin is now a best-selling author, world-renowned speaker, and, of course, an anomaly. The key—he didn't wait to get started.

Having a portfolio of all of the work you have done in the past is important for any brand. It gives people an idea of the types of people you work with, and the type of work you can actually do. People trust real-life examples of a verbal acknowledgement or description.

-------------- Roadmap --------------

1. Sign up for a HARO account.
2. Add to your Anomaly Method Roadmap by documenting the questions that are asked on HARO that fit you and how you answered them so you can copy and paste in the future.

Chapter 27

HOW TO SHOWCASE
YOUR PORTFOLIO

An anomaly is someone getting out and telling their story, or the story of how they accomplished or failed at something. Look at the top brands—they have characters (or personalities behind the brand) sharing what they do, what makes them different, and even behind-the-scenes looks at production. Because of smartphones, having better cameras and access allows almost everyone who has access to create content and share it with the world.

Too often brands shy away from sharing who they are or what they're working on for a number of reasons, ranging from fear of someone stealing the concept, simple insecurity, or fear that they aren't good enough. Start documenting and sharing what you're working on or have worked on in the past. Let go of the reasons why you don't share and start getting your content out there! This content is great for search engines, plus your customers and fans are stoked because they get more from the brand they love!

Let's say you're a design agency who provides graphic design for businesses all across the world. You want to showcase what you can do so others can see it. By creating a portfolio page on your site or social media pages, you accomplish two things: You're supporting and promoting your clients, and you get an opportunity to claim credit for and show off your work to more than just the clients you created it for.

Using the graphic design example on your portfolio page, create case studies that share who your client is, what they were looking for, and what problems you solved for them with your designs. You want to have all of the actual text copy on your website, as search engines index this information, causing your site to come up in search results for the keywords used on the page. For example, if one of your projects used terms like "brand identity," "color theory," and "typography," your site would start to come up for people who search for those terms.

You can also add videos, images, interviews, or any content from the project to help tell the story. This is truly a win-win for you and your client. You help them get a link on your site, which helps them be seen, and in return you get to promote the work you've done. One additional piece of information that can help is using numbers where possible.

Take this for example: "Before working with XYZ Agency, 100 people were visiting their website daily. After we partnered with them to provide graphic design, we helped them get over 1,000 daily views." People love your work and now you have data to put confidence behind it.

Another example of documenting or promoting could be if you have built or are building a product of some kind. Without showing off your "secret sauce" that can be stolen, create a video series of you building the product. Amusement parks do this with time-lapses of roller coasters being built or capping off the top of their first descent.

Content can be anything. The key is getting it from only being seen by you and your team to now being seen by the eyes and ears of your followers and prospects. People buy from people they like and admire. The more they can learn about you, your process, and the behind-the-scenes, the better your chances that they'll like you and therefore buy from you.

Make a list of what you do daily to see what could be a good fit to show the world. It can be things as insignificant, or as silly, as opening the mail when you're getting fan love, or opening a package containing the final piece for the product you're building. Some companies share products that are getting picked up, or, if you're a small business, going to the post office to ship a product. Document what you're doing and share it with the world! You'd be surprised how many people enjoy watching these kinds of things!

Ever go to a conference? What do vendor booths give out? Pens, keychains, stickers, and other little promotional items. Why? They want to be on your mind (whether you realize it or not) and for others to be thinking about them as they look at these items you carry around. Pretty genius marketing. For a few bucks, a business can purchase swag to help promote their business. Same goes with clothing. People promote the brands they love. But, what can you do to promote your business somewhere else? Sure, you can go to a convention and become a vendor, but that's expensive. Rather, how can you get your logo on your customers' websites and in their marketing material?

Next time you're driving, look at the license plate in front of you. What's wrapped around it? Likely a plate cover or sticker with the dealership information of where the car was purchased. Every dealership adds their marketing on every car they sell. It's free advertising for them and most people don't realize it's there or ever think to remove it. So, every car sold drives around town advertising their business. It's cheap for the dealership; they buy tens of thousands at a bulk price and in return get about a decade of advertising done for them with no extra effort on their part.

The License Plate Method is getting your branding on your customers. It's easy to implement. Take an inventory of your current and past clients and reach out to see what their marketing material looks like. They likely are using a short list of the clients they've worked with in the past. If you don't see yours on there, reach out and request they add it. Chances are there's no real reason you weren't included in the first place. A simple request could turn into a bunch of extra exposure for your brand.

And if you happen to build websites, add "Built by Your Company Name" in the footer along with a link back to your site. If someone is hesitant to agree to this, incentivize them with a discount or a percentage of any sale that comes from the link.

A script to reach out to current clients:

Hey brand,

Thanks for choosing us as your vendor. As a token of our appreciation, we'd love to do a case study on your business to be featured throughout our marketing. We will do all the work, all we need is your approval. We'd love it if you could mention us on your website and collateral as well. And, it's a win-win since we provide you 10% of any business that comes our way from you.

Best,

Zack

If you want to be seen in the world, you *must* put your brand everywhere. On a car bumper, a sticker on a computer, a logo on a website, etc. The more eyeballs on your brand, the more exposure you'll get.

Teresa Denham was on her way to a Virginia Tech football game when she realized she didn't have any spirit on her clothing. Instead of buying an overpriced item of clothing on campus, she decided to make something. She didn't go to college and didn't expect to go back to a game, so she didn't need to spend a fortune on spirit swag. She bought some knit gloves and some yarn and sewed pompoms on the fingertips. She called it Spirit Fingerz and people around her continued to ask what she was wearing. Denham contemplated the concept for months until finally she got a patent for the product. She started small—with Virginia Tech colors—and grew a fan base of several thousand in her first year.

By year three, her business made over a million dollars annually with licensing for the NFL and 150 other colleges and universities. Denham, an anomaly, solved the problem of school spirit on gloves. Since her product is unique, it got the attention of others. During her journey into her now decade-old business, Denham understood that if she wanted to be seen, she had to pick up the phone and introduce herself. If you're afraid to pick up the phone, Denham says try to imagine you're someone else when you call or role play. This eases anxieties when making these kinds of calls. During her time in the business, she got a call from Walmart, who wanted her product in their stores. To think she started with just a pair of gloves at a Virginia Tech football game and is now getting calls from one of the largest retailers in the world. Talk about being an anomaly! Denham now leverages her decade of experience and existing network into landing each new deal.

People love to be able to see the work you have done for others. It makes you more approachable. So having a good portfolio is essential. What's even better than a good portfolio? Good testimonials. If you can get your past clients to praise you, the next client will be even easier to land.

-------------- **Roadmap** --------------

1. Take an inventory of the work you have developed for yourself or your clients.
2. Select three examples and document the process.
3. Analyze the results using quantifiable numbers.
4. Where can you put your logo and link on your customers' and fans' websites? Think license plates and stickers.

Chapter 28

ASKING FOR TESTIMONIALS

A former or current client who promotes and endorses you is like making it to the top of K2 or Mount Fuji. It's a big deal. Want to hear something crazy though? Hardly anyone promotes their endorsements or testimonials! When you shop on Amazon or any ecommerce site and you're unsure about the product, what do you do? You read reviews. Once you're convinced one way or another, then you decide. But those are based on social reviews, which are different than testimonials. Unlike a social review on Amazon, Google, Yelp, or Facebook, with a testimonial and endorsements you can control how and where you place them. Instead of having a range of negative to positive reviews, you can solely promote the positive ones, or, if you're a risk-taker, only the negative reviews! There's a lot of ways that you can make this more personal and creative as well. Not just, "Hey we love this product!"

As mentioned in the portfolio promotion chapter, reaching out and notifying your current and past clients to let them know that you would love to do a case study on them is a wonderful start. To begin, make a list of all your clients. If you have thousands, pick a few you know will give you rock-star reviews. Don't just pick one style or industry. Diversify your portfolio of client testimonials. If you

> ## Our revenue just went through the roof because of this. Best decision I've ever made!
> ### - *Jane Doe*
> CEO, Company

work with Walmart and Bob's Local Retail Shop, promote both. You don't want to scare off a potential customer who thinks you're too big to work with them because you work with Walmart.

With testimonials, you want to showcase your big and small clients, different industries, and be diverse in your standard demographics—like age, gender, and race—so you can appeal to all groups in your promotions.

Once you have compiled a diverse list of your current or past customers, think about how you want to incorporate them into your marketing. Case studies, interviews, and showcases are a few ideas. Items typically recommended for these kinds of promotions include a picture of the person providing the quote, a copy of their testimonial, and links back to their site(s). Again, you want this to be win-win. You get love and they get love, too. Ideally, you'll put these testimonials throughout your website and printed marketing material. Show people you're trustworthy, reliable, and worth their time and money. The more often you can have someone else say this for you, the better.

A clever tip to get better results with testimonials is to go deeper on your diversity and look through your customer relationship management system (CRM) or customer list to see what type of title your customers use. It might be Marketing Automation Specialist, Social Media Guru, Founder, President, or HR Manager.

Once you've found the title, be sure to use it in your description and titling of your testimonials.

A potential script to request a testimonial or endorsement could be:

Hey client,

It's been a blast working with you and seeing your product/service/ business grow. We'd love to feature you on our site and through our channels. Can you provide a sentence or two about your experience working with us? We would greatly appreciate it!

Thanks,

Zack

Months go by sometimes and you begin to wonder what you did wrong. Most likely you did nothing wrong and everything right. Some people struggle with what exactly to say when they give a testimonial. Instead of twiddling your thumbs and waiting on them for a response, be proactive right from the get-go. Pay attention in your meetings with clients. If they make a statement that is positive about your business, like, "Wow! You really helped me understand this like no one else has" or "Without you helping me through this really tough time I think my business would have failed," simply take a note of the quote and when the time is right ask them if it's okay to use it.

When is the time right? Hard to say, it may be right then and there, but it also may be sometime down the road. Just recall the quote for them and ask permission to use it on your collateral. Out of courtesy, provide them an opportunity to edit or expand on the quote if they so desire.

Once you have the quote and permission to use it, find places on your website and other sources to promote the endorsement. If you push on social media, be sure to tag the company and person, as it'll improve the chances they engage back with a comment or share.

On your website, create a testimonial page that displays all of the testimonials and then select different ones to place throughout your website, on email signatures, blog posts, and wherever you may promote your business.

Sometimes an endorsement, or testimonial, can be the difference between someone becoming your customer and not. The praise of a stranger can go a long way in helping you get new customers. Think about Amazon. Do you know any of the people who have given reviews on the products you purchase? There's probably a good chance you don't, but you buy based on reviews. So, let this work for you too. One step even further on your endorser is to provide their contact information for someone to call them (assuming they give you permission to do so), just like you would when providing a reference for a job application.

Allan Branch is the co-founder of Less Everything, a software company that creates brands that stick out. Branch believes that there's no "aha" moment or time when your marketing will go viral. He believes you should create, be nice, and slowly you'll start seeing results. Ten years later, you'll think, *"Wow, what a crazy world I have created for myself."* Instead of trying to define success as millions of followers, Branch wants his friends to set goals lower on the bar since he believes they'll be more successful that way.

Throughout the years his business, Less Everything, has not always spoken the way others tend to. The status quo is not something Less is interested in. For example, they would use a Mr. T image on their 404 Error pages with an impersonator saying, "I pity the fool." How clever and memorable is that?

Less Everything created an accounting software, Less Accounting, where their tagline wasn't what the other accounting companies would share. Instead of "Small Business Accounting Made Easy," Less Accounting's tagline was "All Accounting Sucks, We Just Suck Less."

He would get messages from prospects who said the messaging was wrong and unprofessional. Instead of worrying about trying to please them, he would simply smile and say thank you. He didn't try to sway them into becoming a customer. And that is exactly what most business owners do, try to please everyone. If you're trying to please everyone, stop reading this book, throw it away (actually, give it to a friend), and start watching some Oprah videos. If you want to be the anomaly, you must realize that you'll have to be different, you'll stand out, and you *won't* please everyone. Keep reminding yourself that it's okay since the people you'll please are those who'll become customers and raving fans for life.

To get his target customers, or his friends as he calls them, to take notice, Branch talked about being fat or would wear fun socks. While at conferences, he'd go up to strangers and ask them to go to lunch. Instead of thinking of your Twitter followers and your network, focus on creating more relationships when you're at conferences or other networking events. Who couldn't use more friends in their life?

Less Everything, when thinking about what style of marketing works, thinks about whether it's something that seems cool, if it'll break the bank or close the business, and if it's fun. If it doesn't meet those indicators, they never do it. For a business with over a decade of experience to have always at least broken even, they seem to be onto something good.

Being the anomaly is also about breaking social boundaries; if you follow what everyone else is doing, you'll continue to be a follower. Anomalies are not followers. When Branch searched for a conference to attend, he struggled to find one that he considered to be fun. He believes he is a killer storyteller. He wanted to present and share what his friends were doing, so in 2009 he launched LessConf. It felt natural to him to start a conference, and it didn't kill the bank. They were able to bring their friends together and share.

He brought in names that today are synonymous with success, but in 2009 were just getting started—like Gary Vaynerchuk, an entrepreneur, author, speaker, and Internet personality with over 1 million followers on Twitter; Jason Fried, the founder of Basecamp; and Derek Sivers, founder of CD Baby.

Instead of having a huge conference center with crazy overhead, he hosted LessConf in a downtown theater. At the event, there were numerous things that would be considered very odd to outsiders, but to his attendees, they couldn't stop engaging, taking pictures, and wanting more. There was everything from bold T-shirts to odd free games, like a hugging contest onstage for prizes. His philosophy is that if you take the silly and pair it with quality, people will fall in love with you and remain loyal customers for life.

The attendees raved about the events during and after. Branch leveraged their excitement and recorded video testimonials of his guests. He then created a compilation video as a way to entice guests to buy tickets for the next year. Branch understood that he was catering to a very specific crowd, techies, and that if he had 200 raving fans screaming out how great his conference was that he could get more attendees if he showcased their excitement. Attendees would use the word "love" when explaining the conference and how different this conference was than others. Something Branch knew his prospects craved.

When you speak to your target customers in the language they're used to speaking, it's easier for them to consume what you're saying. This tactic of learning the linguistics of your target audience can be used on your website or collateral. Instead of speaking broadly, create specific pages or landing pages geared toward your specific customers. For example, you don't want to sell meat to a vegan, so don't have content or copy associated with meat if you know your targets are vegan. If you have two different target customers who use your products or services differently, make sure you make those distinctions when marketing to each group.

Similar to testimonials from past clients, social reviews can have significant impact on your brand—both good and bad. Learning from the bad reviews and promoting the good ones is a great strategy that'll help your business grow. In the next section, you'll learn how to get more positive reviews online, and what to do with them once you get them.

-------------- **Roadmap** --------------

1. Look through your list of past clients on the AMR document and ask for a testimonial.
2. Pull out similar keywords for titles.
3. Add testimonials to all collateral and your content calendar.

Chapter 29

PROMOTING SOCIAL REVIEWS

As discussed in the previous chapter, a total stranger can be what sells a new customer on your product or service. However, unlike with an endorsement or testimonial, a social review has all types of responses and can even range from insanely positive to horrifically negative. If a prospective customer is on the fence about purchasing what you're selling, they often look through social media reviews and make their decision based on previous customers' experiences.

A social media review is a ranking and sometimes written thoughts about a business, location, or brand. Most ranking sites use a five-star indicator and the ability for its reviewer to explain their reasoning behind the review. There's no rubric or standard. It's purely subjective. If you own a dive bar and it's the best dive bar in the world with the greatest atmosphere, service, and food around, you still could get a less than positive ranking because of the stigma attached to being a dive bar. It's imperative that context of the customer's experience is included to understand why a review is what it is. If it was a great review, what made it possible for the customer to have a great experience? If it was a dismal review, how did it happen? Social reviews can go a long way in telling potential customers whether or not they should give your business a shot.

Social media reviews should be encouraged, and there are several ways to request them. No matter what kind of a review you receive, see it as a way to learn from your customers in a form where they feel comfortable. Not everyone wants to tell their waiter at a restaurant that the food was terrible. It's human nature to be concerned with hurting someone's feelings. Typically, most people comment about their experiences online after the fact. It would then be up to you to learn from the response and to get in touch with the person who provided the review.

For good reviews, ask what made them enjoy their experience. Then double down on those areas. If you own a retail shop and the reviewer says they enjoyed how the sales staff weren't pushy and gave them some space to shop, relay that message to your sales staff.

For bad reviews, ask for specifics on what could have been better. Get as many details as possible, and then invest time in improving those areas.

Keep in mind that not all customers are the same. Not everyone enjoys or dislikes the same things about their experience with your brand, so don't make enormous changes based on one person's input. Take note, but don't implement anything until you see a pattern emerge.

Additionally, some businesses use an incentive to increase their reviews—giveaways, discounts, exclusive access to VIP events, you name it. The more reviews a business has, the better their pages rank in social media. The algorithms behind the social media ranking platforms want engagement, so the more that people rank or review a page, the better the chance of that business being seen, and seen often, on social media sites.

Just note that not all reviewers have actually been customers, which could provide you with inaccurate data. If you're getting reviews because you're giving away a car, you can expect people are giving reviews to win that car. They may never have been customers in the past and may never become one either.

With billions of consumers on their cellphones these days, accidents do happen. I once received a one-star review without any information on my Facebook page. It was odd. I looked through my CRM for this person's name, but it didn't come up. Instead of letting it go, I reached out to this individual to learn about their experience. During the dialogue, it was revealed that it was an accident and somehow the one star was hit on a mobile phone. The individual, not familiar with the business, deleted the ranking. Similar scenarios have happened several times now with the same story and outcome each time, so be sure to follow up with any negative reviews, especially if they don't have any explanation.

Learn why people are leaving the reviews they do. Social media is supposed to be social, a two-way street. If they're doing exactly what you want them to do, engage! You should and *must* engage back. Otherwise you're wasting your time and probably shouldn't even have a social media account.

Reach out individually to each reviewer and introduce yourself. Let them know you have seen the review and want to learn more about their experience. People love knowing that they're appreciated. If you run a social media page, publicly respond to every review. If it's a serious matter, don't go into a battle back and forth as the public will see it.

All too often, people are emotional train wrecks and they regret their social posts in the coming days. You don't want your negative comments on a bad review to change the minds of your raving fans. Everyone and every business has bad days. It's how you learn from it that will help you prosper in the future.

If you have yet to receive reviews on your business page, first ensure that you have accounts on Google, Yelp, Facebook, and other ranking sites. Most sites are free and easy to set up. Once you do, reach out to your current customers and ask them to leave a public review. Depending on the site, you can add location, hours, description, images, and several other key metrics. These sites are popular and often rank higher in search engines than your website, which isn't a bad thing. Think of it as an opportunity to let your fans tell others how they feel about you. If your profiles are set to win as described earlier in this book, you should have no problem landing new customers. You can look at these big sites as partners where you may not have the ability to add features to your website. Sites like Yelp have a ton of useful features for customers that you may not be able to build out on your own site for whatever reason—things like a built-in map with directions, a viewable menu, customer photos, direct contact information, etc. A strong social media page can be engaging, beneficial, and an opportunity to land business, even if you don't have a website.

To increase reviews, brick-and-mortar stores often have leave-behinds, like business cards, coupons, and flyers asking for reviews from their customers. Typically, there's an incentive for a free item or discount at a future visit. Encouraging visitors to review helps you and it is easy to offer them an opportunity to do so during their experience.

A script to use is similar to the testimonial script.

Hey clients or fans,

We love you and love being able to help you. We're working to increase our exposure on (insert social media ranking platform) and would love if you would provide us a review of our business. It would mean the world to us! For one lucky reviewer, we're offering one free item of their choice, but the review must be in by 10/17. Thanks so much for your help!

Thanks,

Zack

If you aren't convinced how these reviews can help you, the next time you buy something think about the experience that made you finally say yes. Your decision to buy probably had a lot more to do with an anonymous review than you might have realized.

Brock Hogan went on a business trip and visited an escape room. Intrigued, he looked into bringing a franchise to his hometown. The franchise fees were way more than he thought they should be, so he decided to open one on his own. Now the owner of two escape rooms, Hogan has racked up a savvy business and hundreds of thousands of raving fans, all who get to play a real-life game of Clue. One of his biggest techniques is leveraging his social media reviews to gain future customers. Hogan states, "A social review is important because it draws eyes and attention to your business that would otherwise not be seen."

People go to platforms like Facebook and Google looking for certain businesses. When they find you and your competitors on the initial landing page, everyone looks the same. Social reviews are what will differentiate you from your competitors.

It's important for you to not only be on these platforms, but also have positive reviews and positive experiences that people are sharing because that's going to help people make decisions about doing business with you. Hogan understands if he finds fun ways to get reviews, it can help get new business, even if that means not directly asking for a review but letting it happen organically. The reality, as Hogan says, is that not only do good reviews help you, but negative ones can as well. You can use them as a learning experience.

On the footer of their escape room websites, they have social media icons, signs in their lobby showcase previous guests' experiences, as well as a reminder after the game is played that if they share their experience on social media it helps them grow their business. People inherently want to help grow a business that they love and have had a great experience with.

When they get a bad review, Hogan wants to know why. But, he understands that he must first understand the context of the review and that sometimes he can't fix everything. If there's something that they can improve upon, like staffing issues, he wants to fix it. If you're on the fence about pushing for a review, he says that in a world of Facebook, Instagram, Google, etc., people are people. People like to be the center of influence within their circle. So, when they share these things and experiences, it shows their sphere of influence what they're up to and what they think about it. Keep in mind that in many cases, reviews of our competitors are also helpful for us because we can learn from what they're doing, see pictures of what customers went through, and see ways that we can improve.

If you want to be the anomaly, Hogan says you must be conscious of the customer experience from the time that the customer pulls into the parking lot until they leave, ensuring that the process is the same every time. If you can dedicate a team member to social reviews, even if it's a few minutes a day, you have a much better chance of ensuring you get reviews.

Nate Tschohl was on the swim team throughout his childhood and into his teen years. When he became an adult, the next logical step for him was to become a coach. He ended up coaching with his best friend and while coaching created a network of friends in the swimming world. For several years, Tschohl tweeted about swimming-related events, whether it was big meets, the Olympics, Michael Phelps, or even swimming deaths. He became a known entity on Twitter as an advocate for swimming. With millions of impressions a month, he built his new community. He called it swimnerd (for which the logo is a swimmer in nerdy glasses). While he was grateful for his following, he didn't know what else to do other than continue to develop that following.

He often pondered his time as a coach, specifically remembering the archaic clocks used by the swim world. Instead of continuing to let it slide, he investigated whether or not he could develop a better clock. He didn't have the skills to build a swim clock, but he had a community of followers who were interested in a clock that would work easier for swim practices, especially if it was at 75 percent of the cost of the old ones. He created a Kickstarter campaign and asked his following to contribute. He raised over $60,000 in 30 days. As he learned the process of turning a community into a business, he traveled to several manufacturing plants across the globe to ultimately see which one was best. As his clocks began to ship, swimnerd began to receive unsolicited reviews and ratings online.

Tschohl believes reviews are the most important thing prospective customers use to make their purchasing decisions. Thus, they're critical to success. They provide a stamp of approval, and Tschohl and his team use their social media reviews in prominent places on their website and product pages, as well as in their advertising and email marketing. They believe in social proof so much that they even put the reviews before the actual product specs.

The best place to be is everywhere—on audio, visual, video, and social media. One of the most popular platforms is podcasting. It's one of the easiest to start, which can be good and bad—good since you can launch right now and start getting new visitors; bad because everyone else can too! But if you think like an anomaly, you can quickly differentiate your podcast from every other Joe Schmoe out there (no offense if your name is Joe Schmoe).

-------------- Roadmap --------------

1. Go through your current social media platforms and engage with any previous reviews (i.e., Like and comment on each, even if they are bad. Do not go on a tirade with negative comments.)
2. Create a post asking your followers to review your business, podcast, or brand.
3. Individually reach out to followers and ask them to provide you a review.
4. Design graphics promoting top reviews; if you do not have a graphic designer on staff, try Canva. Add social reviews to your content calendar.

5. Actively display top reviews from your most influential and diverse following throughout your physical and online collateral.

Chapter 30

LANDING PODCAST INTERVIEWS

P odcasts are the new radio. However, unlike radio, you can choose what you want to listen to ahead of time, and at your leisure.

If you like Howard Stern or Tim Ferris and only want to listen to them, with radio there are commercials and dead zones. With podcasts, you have the ability to catch and grasp content in audio form (and sometimes video) from a preselected author. There are over 1 million podcasts worldwide with billions of total listens. Yes, billions. Statistics show that 44 percent of the U.S. population has listened to a podcast—49 percent at home and 22 percent in a vehicle—with 80 percent listening to the majority of an episode. People are mobile, and podcasts fill that need. So why not use it to your advantage?

Like other mediums, you must get your content on your site to make sure that you control your marketing. That's the key. If you wait for the publisher of the content you were interviewed for, the podcast host, or even a media agency, you could be waiting weeks, months, or even years! That's crazy. You must take control of the marketing of you. You can't hope that the publisher of your best podcast interview will promote you over and over again. That is your job.

In this section, you'll learn how to start a podcast, how to be interviewed on someone else's podcast, and how to meet anyone you want by using the Fraternity of Podcast Guests Method.

Creating a podcast is easy, but most podcasts never get to episode seven. Why? People quit. If you're interested in starting a podcast, you'll need a microphone, editing software, a podcast host, and a topic. That's it. Now, the fancier you want to get with it, the more expensive it gets. But, you can get it off the ground for less than $100 (assuming you already have or have access to a computer or smartphone). Not bad! If you're okay with going super raw, you can use a voice memo app on your cellphone and a microphone, but if you want to bring guests onto the podcast and they don't live close enough to come to you, you'll have to invest in a couple pieces of recording equipment.

Here's an example. Let's say you own a car-detailing shop and want to create a show for car enthusiasts. Makes sense, you talk about cars, car enthusiasts like cars, they learn about you, that you own a car-detailing shop, and they become a customer without you even pitching your business to them.

Make your listeners fall in love with you and what you do. Bring on some cool guests and the next thing you know, you're a podcast host with new business coming your way potentially from every episode! Once you have your podcast up, you can use the methods in this book to grow your following. Maybe you don't want to start a podcast and would rather be interviewed on someone else's podcast. This is a great and easy way to get your name out for free. And, unlike the traditional media we discussed, it's a lot easier to get on a podcast than it is to get featured in a story.

To find a podcast you want to be interviewed on, start searching the podcast stores, iTunes and Google Play, to start. Read descriptions of the different shows and then listen to some of them to see if it's a good fit for you. Most podcasts have a "Do you want to be on the show?" form. Fill out the form and put your name in the hat. If you don't raise your hand and say pick me, you'll never be picked.

Most podcasts ask similar profiling questions on their forms: Who you are? What you have done? Why should you be on the show? Spend some time crafting a message that is compelling and then don't hesitate—send it! If you don't get asked to be on the show, no sweat, just find another show. Create a document with all of the shows you're pitching, as well as the questions they asked and your answers. Don't use the exact same wording for each one. You can use the same content but tweak each time you send it to a new show. Remember, the bigger the podcast, the more difficult it'll be to get on the show. But there are several B- and C-size podcasts that have a significant following and would love to have you.

Once they've recorded and aired the episode with your interview, get a copy and embed it on your site. Yes, this is legal. If you're unfamiliar, most podcast players allow anyone to copy the contents of an episode and paste it on a forum or website. The original content is still owned by the podcast, however, you're able to create a story around your episode. Ideally you'll create a new blog post telling the story of the episode while tempting guests to listen to it. Once the page is optimized, schedule it with your posting tool.

The Fraternity of Podcast Guests Method is a concept I came up with a few years ago. I define it as the group of all of the other people who have been guests on the same podcast as you. You can leverage a common connection and create a relationship from it. If you're an alumnus of a university or college, it's the same thing. You can be brand new to a city but have a connection to someone who went to the same school you did, even if it was decades ago.

How can you find your fraternity of podcast guests? As you begin to make the podcast tour, simply look at the list of people who have also been on the podcast and introduce yourself.

> Hey John,
>   I see you were on Johnny Jay's podcast! Awesome, so was I. I wanted to introduce myself. I enjoyed your episode.
>   Best,
>   Zack

Yes, an introduction email can be that simple. Have you ever been to a bar or some large facility and found someone who was an alum of your school? The connection automatically occurs. Even though you have no idea who the person is, you feel an immediate connection with them since you both went to the same school. Podcast fraternities can produce a similar experience.

You can sometimes find their contact information on the podcast page, but you may have to do some digging. Try searching Google to see what pops up. It could be their website, LinkedIn profile, or another site featuring them. Search through in that order until you find their contact information. If you can't find specific contact information, a LinkedIn request will do the trick, but you only have a few characters to get the message across. So, make sure you don't send them a TL;DR.

To go even deeper, you can introduce yourself and tell them you have shared their episodes with your network and following. People love it when their story is shared!

Brandon T. Adams is a crowdfunding expert and the voice behind the *Live to Grind* podcast, a hit show that inspires its listeners to become successful in life and in business. Early in his career, Adams Googled his name and found an actor with the same name. Knowing it would be difficult to pop up in searches ahead of *The Mighty Ducks* and *The Sandlot* star, he added his middle initial to his common-day use of his name. Besides the fact that it works when people search for him, it sets him apart since few people use their middle initial. On top of that, when he started his podcast, he traveled to each of his guests, even if that meant driving cross-country! This made his guests feel incredibly valued and they liked him even more. In a world with tens of thousands of popular podcasts, Adams knew he had to do something to stand out. Now he has hundreds of interviews under his belt, including *Shark Tank* shark and As Seen On TV founder Kevin Harrington, YouTube star Jake Paul, and popular podcaster John Lee Dumas. Adams started *Live to Grind* to build up his reputation and influence. He also did it to create an avenue to connect with other influencers and provide them value by giving them an interview on his podcast.

Another one of the most popular ways to use your expertise to become known is by writing blog posts. Blog posts are probably the easiest way to start creating content. All you need is a computer, or access to one.

-------------- **Roadmap** --------------

1. What is your show about? Determine the topic of your podcast using keywords and what you love. If you do not want to start a podcast, use your answers as a guide to get onto others' podcasts.
2. What makes your show/you unique? What are five things that make you stand out?
3. Who is your target guest? What shows do you want to be interviewed on? Add these guests/shows to your AMR.
4. In a sentence: Who are you?
5. Go through your list of contacts and determine who you have ties to using the Fraternity of Podcast Guests Method and introduce yourself to all parties included. If you have your own show and they fit the bill, invite them onto your show. If you do not, simply introduce yourself and just say, "Hey."

Chapter 31

HOW TO LEVERAGE BLOG POSTS

As you know by now, putting yourself out there is critical to becoming an anomaly. If you stay in your safe little cave, no one will ever find you. But, if you're visible, people will find you and you'll make a name for yourself or business. This is why you're reading *Anomaly*, right?!

Content is king. Finding the right medium that you feel comfortable with is important. If you like to be on camera or out on the main stage, then videos and podcasts are likely your thing. Perhaps, though, you enjoy writing as opposed to video or audio. Do what makes you feel the most comfortable, because being uncomfortable does you no favors in relaying your content to the world.

Blog content is a crucial way to get your message out for three reasons:

- It indexes well with search engines.
- It's easy for people to consume.
- You can have a melting pot of content and stories all under your roof or website.

In this chapter, you'll be introduced to blogging, how to do it, what to blog about, how to get your messages out, and how to be visible from day one. Blogging is simply producing written content. Even if your preference is audio and/or video, create content that is rich in text for search engine purposes. Search engines can't read a video or audio file to know what it says. So, don't skip over this chapter as it's a critical component to getting your message out into the world.

Could you come up with twenty-five blog posts? If you the answer is no, you need to do more research or broaden your approach. A steady flow of content is critical when trying to grow your audience.

A blog post is broken into several layers: a headline or title, opening statement, the body or story, closing statement, tags, description, and sources. Just like a newspaper, a headline is the single most important layer of a blog post. You can have the greatest blog post in the world, but if your headline sucks and is not compelling, no one will ever read the post. Headlines are an art. There are many headline tools to help you improve your opportunity to get a click or a visitor to continue reading. If visitors are not interested in your headline, they'll move on. A headline is just as important as the post itself when you're promoting the blog on social media. Typically, they're short, definite, and entice the reader to learn more. This doesn't mean to lie just to get someone to click. This is called clickbait and the Internet hates it. I'm sure you understand if you have ever clicked an intriguing story link only to find out the actual content has zero correlation to the headline that captured your attention.

For practice, pick up a newspaper, or head to your favorite content website, and see what stories hook you. Copy down what they say and dissect them. Oftentimes a headline with a lot of reads is one that is the "exception to the rule." For example, P90X, the popular video training program, promotes that you can lose 50 pounds in a few short months with their program. Some people have lost that weight, so this isn't false information, but if you don't put in the work and follow their outline, results are unlikely. If you were a sports reporter for the New England Patriots, a headline that would get hits would be "Brady Throws Over 500 Yards and Loses." As you get started with headlines, send a few to your best readers and ask them to choose between a few of their favorites. It's a good measure of what other readers may gravitate toward, too.

Once you have a headline, think about outlining your content. Start with a thesis statement and then break it down into a series of paragraphs that reinforce your thesis statement, sprinkling in interviews and other sources to help strengthen and support your thesis. Wrap it up with a closing paragraph that backs up your thesis statement. To make your content more compelling, be sure to add images and videos with tags. If you look at the structure of popular articles, they also use different styles and sizes of fonts. This is a good idea to use for SEO (search engine optimization), as it indexes your headlines and paragraph titles for keywords. Those keywords make it easier for a search engine to find you, thus making it easier for customers to find you. The better a job a blog post does of using keywords, the higher it ranks in a search engine. When you're writing your blog post, be sure to think of the one or two keywords or phrases that you want this post to be about, so you give your post its best chance at a high ranking.

If you provide training for soccer athletes, your keywords would be something about soccer and training. You can use a search engine's analytics to understand what keywords people are searching for to find you. You can also look at a comparable website and see what keywords they're using to get attention. While you may not know the exact keywords to use, you should be able to get a good idea based on what they're using. A keyword is almost always in a headline and throughout the blog post. If the blog post shows its tags, you should be able to find them there.

Another great way to rank higher is to have links to sources that you mention in your article. If there's an article explaining "How to Write Better Content," this could be sourced and linked for this sentence. If your content gets linked to popular websites, it's likely to move up in the search engine rankings.

There's no set length for a blog post, but many search engines rank lengthier blog posts higher than shorter ones. Search engines like to have a lot of words. Some say posts should have 1,000 words. However, the average post on WordPress is just 280 words long. Do what feels like the best fit for your content. Don't make it long for the sake of doing so. That'll water down your content and it won't be as enticing to readers. On the flip side, don't cut out important material just to make it a quick read. Write as much information as you can while keeping it all relevant and interesting.

To get your blog posts seen, be sure to send them to your closest friends, family, and followers and encourage them to share it with their networks. If your website is still new and you're learning how to get eyeballs on your content, consider using blogging distribution tools that are searchable and indexable platforms, such as Medium.

Medium is an online publishing platform that allows authors to write and post content while it acts as the distributor. It's similar to a blog, however, the content doesn't sit on your website, it sits on Medium. This is a risky technique, as you're not sending people to your own site or a platform that you control. But, if you get shared by an industry influencer, it could be seen by millions and go viral.

Chris Hill, a chef from Atlanta, GA, spent months working on content around inspiring chefs, cooks, and the staff in the back of the house at restaurants. He wrote on Medium and had several hundred views for every blog post. One day, he woke up to 500 emails from other chefs who read his article. His view rate was also up to 5,000.

This quickly turned into millions of views just because he decided to put his story out there. He added an email subscribe link at the end of the article and a Facebook page link and now thousands follow him. With over 150,000 Facebook likes, Hill has gone on to speak at TEDx, has written several books, secures paid speaking gigs on a regular basis, and is a proven thought leader in the culinary world—an anomaly.

He wasn't writing content around recipes and which food goes with what. Instead, he experienced how negative the restaurant world was and wanted to share feedback and inspiration to fix that. He received letters from his followers outlining how he changed their lives. Someone who had contemplated suicide even told him he saved their life.

In the early 2010s, Jason Vitug was ready to step out and create his own content around financial literacy. Vitug, who at the time was a corporate VP, took his skills and his network and created Phroogal, an online content directory of information for those looking to improve their financial well-being. When he started, he was a nobody. So, he reached out to his family and friends and asked them to subscribe to his newsletter, in which he would keep them up to date on the content that he was writing. This small group of 100 was excited to hear from him and was willing to help share his content as he developed it. Vitug learned that his network was willing to help him, but he had to remind them first that the content existed. Now, he travels the United States and provides a financial tour to 50-plus communities every year called The Road to Financial Wellness Road Trip.

Kickstarter, the leading crowdfunding platform, is filled with people starting projects of all kinds and looking to receive early funding from adopters in exchange for some type of reward. Kickstarter has done a tremendous job creating successful projects. Their end goal is to get more campaigns funded. Knowing that many campaigns fail, they created content around how to build a more successful campaign. This content is visible, marketed, and open to everyone. The more money a campaign funds, the more money Kickstarter makes, so it's in their best interest to help a campaign succeed. It's a win-win for everyone involved.

If you have a high-performing blog post that people like, think about turning it into a webinar or online course. If you're in a specialized industry, hosting a webinar can really help grow your brand and establish you as the authority. You have probably come across at least one webinar or online course. They're typically long-form videos that educate an audience on a specific topic. If the content you provide requires a lot of in-depth education, like car maintenance, then webinars and courses are a good place for you to focus your time and energy. Use the course or webinar as a piece of your sales funnel, with the goal being to eventually turn your guests into paid users of some kind.

-------------- **Roadmap** --------------

1. Start your blog through your own website or through Medium.
2. Compile a list of twenty-five topics. (If you are stuck, think about what questions people often ask you, create top lists or how-tos.)
3. Each topic should be written around a specific keyword or key phrase. Make sure that it's in your headline and throughout the content.
4. Add your content to your content calendar and distribute.

Chapter 32

USING WEBINARS AND COURSES

A webinar allows you to educate your prospects on a process that they're trying to learn more about. In their eyes, you become the authority, and then at the end of the webinar, you upsell your product or service. While you don't have to upsell since you have your target watching you for a long period of time, you should consider it since they now have a vested interest in you and will want more.

Let's say you sell a car-cleaning kit and want to sell more units. Instead of just saying, "Buy my kit," you can produce a webinar. The topics can be how to clean your car, tricks to clean up the spills in your car, or how to turn your dirty rims into shiny wheels that glisten like the Emerald City in *The Wizard of Oz*. Car enthusiasts are constantly working on their cars and looking for new ways to keep them up to date. Give them something useful.

If you went to a conference or trade show, a speaker would take a similar approach in front of a crowd of people. The only difference for you is you'll be recording it instead of speaking live. The goal is to present an idea that can provide at least 45 minutes of content. Seems like a lot of time but the longer you keep someone's attention, the more their trust builds and the greater the likelihood of them purchasing something from you or becoming your follower.

Think about webinars like this: When you find something you want to watch while channel surfing, do you keep changing channels? No. You stop and watch!

Webinars are about education and reputation building. By now, you should have a good idea as to what you're good at. Now it's time to take your blog and social media posts and turn them into a long-form video course.

Develop an outline of what you want the big goal, or outcome, to be for the viewer. What will they now have the ability to do or have more knowledge of by the end? Choose a compelling title that has your keywords and goals included. Next, think about the contents or the body of the webinar. It helps to think of this like chapters in a book. Finally, tie all of these sections together and transition your visitors into your upsell. Even if you're not going to upsell anything, you should at least give them a call to action, such as liking your social media page(s), subscribing to your email list or YouTube Channel, or get them set up for a call for your 50-Ten Challenge. If someone is ready to take action, give them an avenue to do it!

Many webinars are live with the host at a specific time, just like a TV show or the release of a podcast. A webinar has a specific date so you can get bulk views and help more people at one time.

Let's continue with the car-cleaning concept. As a detailer, think about which questions you're often asked. One of those may be "How do I keep my car cleaner for longer?" You turn your ten best techniques to solving this problem into a webinar. Once you're perceived as an expert on how to make their life better, they'll come back to you for help often, tell people in their network about you, and, the ultimate goal, buy from you.

Use the following outline to build your webinar. It may change as you learn more about your viewers' needs:

- Title
- Takeaways
- An introduction to you and why they should trust you
- The contents
- Q&A
- The wrap-up

- The transition
- The upsell
- More Q&A

You'll need the following tools to put together a webinar:

- Access to a computer
- A video camera
- Access to a microphone
- A PowerPoint presentation (if you plan to not be the only thing seen on camera)

Bret Fisher is a specialist in a development tool called Docker. Docker is a computer program that performs operating-system-level virtualization, also known as containerization, which is built by Docker. In 2015, Fisher was intrigued by the tool and started hosting meetups to help others train and become fluent in the language. By hosting meetups, Docker and Fisher created a relationship which led to an opportunity for Fisher to create a deep-dive course for the Docker community. Docker had some content around their platform, but they were not interested in doing a ten-hour course, so they asked Fisher if he would be interested in creating this. Fisher ultimately decided to give it a shot. With many unknowns, Fisher knew that creating this course was risky due to the amount of time and money needed to build it. But he also knew it could have many upsides, including increased revenue, awareness, speaking opportunities, and authority status.

The risk worked out for Fisher. He gets up to 500 new customers a day for his Docker Mastery course (which, by the way, is one of the top courses on the Udemy site). A course is important because one of the best ways to learn something is from someone who has already "been there and done that." Hosting your course on a site like Udemy comes with some downfalls. You take a loss by not receiving the full revenue. From a search engine standpoint, the course site wins over your site, even if it's your content. At the end of the day, your course is generating traffic for the host site. That said, many course sites have budgets that you don't have and awareness that could be worth leveraging their brand instead of your own.

After selling over 40,000 courses over a short nine months, Fisher says there are seven keys to winning at developing a course, one of them being to give away your best content or material. On a site like Udemy, you can preview a series of the course material to get some ideas of this process. The technique is similar to a book on Amazon that shares a few chapters with its readers, often the best chapters. An author could also use this technique on their website to collect emails in exchange for a few top chapters of their book. To grab attention, create a unique title that includes your main keyword. You can also use keywords and buzzwords throughout your copy to improve your searchability. The key for getting a course viewed is its promotional video. You only have seven seconds to get someone to spend more time on your course, so be sure to hook them quickly. Otherwise, they'll move on, which is, of course, not what you want.

Put yourself in the video and tell a story. You want to make sure you say who you are, why you're credible, what customers receive, how easy it'll be for them to consume, what level your course is, and what their takeaways will be after they complete the course.

Courses are similar to what you would do in school, but easier to consume. They don't cost as much or take nearly as long to complete. Since you're learning from a current expert, it's the most up-to-date training instead of potentially outdated material. Before you use a course-hosting platform, be sure to understand how to use it. If you do it your way, you may set yourself up for failure. Read the FAQs, reach out to a few course instructors to see what helped them the best, leverage the concepts from Fisher's Docker Mastery course, and even reach out to those courses that are under-producing to see what they think has not worked for them. The more you can understand before developing and producing your course, the better off you'll be.

With over 7,500 reviews of his course, Fisher leverages a large number of his ratings to help him get his next sale. He even uses them to cheer himself up when he's having a bad day. When he gets a review, he thanks the reviewer and those who provide a longer review he gives a more in-depth response. Remember, if someone provides you feedback, respond and thank them for it.

A course can be broken down into its headline or title; what your students will learn; the curriculum; a short, high-level description of what they will get; who the instructor is; as well as a series of reviews and how many students have taken the course. When getting started, you won't have a large number of students and reviews yet. The key is to get your first one, then a few more, and along the way be sure to provide them the best value and experience possible. This encourages them to give you props through reviews, share it with their friends, and help increase your exposure.

Courses are often thought of as digital video versions of books and they can help you become an authority in your line of work. Having a course is awesome, and marketing it using social media is a great strategy to get new eyeballs on you and off of other content. Social media is an avenue that allows people to network. Engagement and relationship building should be your focus with social media. Social media is a two-way street, so if you intend to only expel information to people and never engage back, you'll struggle to see increases in engagement or "likes" for your page. Your followers want to be valued and if your content focuses on you telling people what to do and it's not engaging, they'll move on to someone else.

-------------- **Roadmap** --------------

1. Determine the content you have created (or you're interested in creating) and create an outline of material similar to a blog post, but that you can dive deeper into and add more details, case studies, and quiz-like material.
2. What is your goal for this content (e.g., a subscribe, a buy, stronger awareness and engagement, etc.)?
3. Determine if you will host on your website or host on a course/webinar platform like Skillshare or Udemy.
4. Create a title.
5. What takeaways will the student receive?
6. Why should a student take your class?
7. Create content.

Chapter 33

OPTIMIZING FACEBOOK

F acebook is the largest social network in the world with over two billion users. While it would be difficult to get all two billion following you (nor would you want them to), you can anticipate getting a slice of that pie. As with other tools described in this book, it's imperative to understand how this tool was built and to use it for its specific purpose.

Facebook has many features, two of which are Groups and Messenger. Groups are one of the most trusted sources of industry-specific information on social media. The moderators are looked at as the authorities for the topic that Group is based on. A Facebook Group is similar to a meetup or conference, only it's digital and doesn't have an end date or time. As with any social media tool, you do have to be cautious since what works today may not work tomorrow. For example, Facebook Groups used to notify members when a new post was added. They've since added a feature allowing members of these Groups the ability to mute notifications. So, if you want to see this content, you have to manually go in and find it. You can do this by turning on post notifications in the groups you desire. If you have not already created a Group, consider starting one and plan twenty-five pieces of content for driving conversations.

Start by naming the Group and inviting your target customers using similar strategies you did for adding prospects to your email lists. If you have a Facebook Page, you can link it to the Group. With a Group, you're trying to get engagement. It doesn't happen because you post—you have to reach out to members, ask what they want or are hoping for in a Group, and then ask them to respond to the post. When Reddit started, the initial team members created fake accounts and had conversations with each other. Now, you don't want to do this, but that example shows that engagement is hard work. Once you have it though, it can be very powerful.

You'll find standard Facebook features like images, videos, and text in Facebook Groups. There's the ability to run polls and set the visibility so that the public can see it, or only the people in the Group. Similar to your editorial calendar, create concepts and campaigns around the topics your viewers want. If you can't get answers from your group members, it doesn't mean they don't want to consume, you just need to have a one-on-one conversation with them outside of the group. Then, take those questions or statements and frame the content around their needs. You can join other groups and see what works for them and what challenges continue to arise and build your group around those.

Not everyone feels comfortable engaging with a Group, even if they're consuming the content. However, the more comfortable your members get within the Group, the more they'll engage, which is what you want. You can help people feel more comfortable by introducing new members or by asking them to introduce themselves to the Group. A general template is:

> "We want to introduce Zack Miller, our newest member of Anomaly Nation (the name of the Group). Zack is the Founder of Hatch, which helps people stand out in a crowded room by being a little different."

By posting this, you're welcoming the new member and sharing what they do with your group. Whether a Facebook Group or any page or distribution platform, this is a great way to promote engagement with a simple introduction.

If you're looking to expand your brand but don't know how, learn from other Groups on Facebook. See what types of content others are requesting and engaging in. Then, create that content and share it with the individuals requesting it. You can also engage with other groups to build up your credibility and authority status. If you're the one constantly answering the questions of others in Groups, they'll look at you as one who has the answers. At that point you can create a new relationship and make it personal with a PM.

Private messaging (or PM) is similar to texting on your phone. Instead of sending through your cellphone carrier, you do so through the platform you're using. With Facebook, you can send messages to anyone whom you would like to create or develop a relationship. The great thing about PM is, instead of broadcasting your conversations to everyone on your Page or Group, you can open a chat window and have a private conversation there. For example, if while perusing Facebook you find that someone is going through a challenge that you can fix, it's probably a better idea to PM them rather than post publicly to the Group. If the person is someone you want to connect with but have never actually met, consider sending them a PM introducing yourself in addition to a friend request. That way they know a little about you and it's not a "cold" request.

Oddly enough, people feel comfortable having PM conversations on Facebook, even if they've never met you before. Be sure to friend request them first. If you don't, the message goes into an alternative folder and the user may never see it. Once they accept your friend request, Facebook notifies you. Introduce yourself with your commonalities.

> *"Hey, I'm Zack and I'm also a member of the Anomaly Nation Facebook Group. I wanted to introduce myself as I have been following your conversation on the page recently and I've really enjoyed what I've read <or> and I think I might have some ideas for you."*

By engaging, you're not being a pushy salesperson. You're introducing yourself and leveraging a common ground where you both feel comfortable communicating. Insert Fraternity of Podcast Guests Method on Facebook. Just like you would when meeting someone at a networking event or for the first time over coffee, just have a conversation. The only difference is you're doing it online instead of in person. Learn about them, what they do for a living, what they enjoy doing in their free time, and find more commonalities and pain points where you can help them. Provide value but respect their time.

On Facebook you can share your content in a variety of ways, but to become the anomaly, you'll need to focus on building premium relationships where your followers turn into raving fans who share your content. One of the biggest hurdles that pages and brands have to overcome is getting people to consistently share their content. A share on Facebook is the single most important action that can occur to promote engagement. Sure, people liking and commenting on your content is great, but if someone shares your content, that means your content is getting in front of their network and the relationships they have with others. This doesn't mean you ask people you don't have a relationship with to straight up share your content with their networks—that strategy rarely works. But, you do need to let people know what action you want them to take. If they comment and engage with your content regularly, take it to PM and create that more personal relationship as described above. Then, politely ask if they would share your content with their network through Facebook. If you don't tell them what you want or need, how do they know to do it? If you want an action to happen—for someone to share your content or buy your product—ask, don't hope.

A simple introduction goes a long way. Set a goal of creating five new relationships a day (or per week, whatever you think is reasonable for you). By the end of a month, you potentially have 150 new relationships, and by the end of a calendar year you could have close to 2,000 new relationships. Rarely will people pop up and reach out to you; instead, be the one who starts the conversation.

Don't forget to engage with other people's content. Remember, it's a two-way street. If you're not engaging with others, there's a good chance they won't end up engaging with you. When you get on Facebook, make it a rule that it's for engagement and new relationship building, not watching kitten and dog videos (okay, not *only* for enjoying kitten and dog videos).

> Nick Sutton is a photographer. He joined a Facebook Group, the *Hampton Roads Photographers Network,* to learn from his peers and when the group's creator moved on, he reached out to him to take over the group. When he took over the Facebook Group, they were just beginning to receive traction. Sutton saw this group as a community and

wanted to help himself and others learn from other photographers in his area about photography best practices.

He says a community is a series of people willing to share information, and who aren't afraid to share their secrets. They know there are enough people out there for everyone to have clients. This helps the group's members to come together within the community.

Many would be threatened by giving up their special sauce to their peers, but Facebook Groups allow collaboration and a true learning experience similar to a mastermind group or a conference, except it's on-demand. When asked about whether or not one should give out all of their secrets, Sutton says, "I don't think you want to give someone 100 percent of the roadmap to success. You want them to learn, to go through the trenches. You don't want to pave an asphalt road and have them skip along their way. You know you want them to figure it out. There are many opportunities for many people. I don't think sharing information is going to hurt you in the long run. It's going to make you seem sincerer and it's going to create a relationship with that person that's going to allow you to not only grow yourself as a photographer, but to help you grow your business."

While Sutton was growing his Facebook Group into the thousands, he learned that many were looking for locations of where they could and should photograph their clients. Most were hush-hush about the topic, so he created a map showing off the top locations on his website Digital Lens Rental. (He owns a local camera rental shop.) He believes the best way to have an engaged group is to ask open-ended questions. He asks questions like, "What's the best lens to use...?" or "What location is a nightmare to photograph?" By asking for engagement without prompting members to comment on the post, the comments have blossomed into hundreds a day. By managing the Group, Nick saw a thread from his members looking for access to rental equipment that wasn't shipped from a factory or that they had to drive hours to get. He owned equipment and decided to open up his shop to rent his equipment. The Facebook Group is one of the largest contributors of deal flow for him, plus it's a free resource for photographers in his community and it provides them value.

To really understand his customers' needs, he polls them as soon as they request access to the group. If they don't meet his standards, they don't get to join. For example, the first question he asks is what type of photographer or talent they are. If they say "other," they're usually someone trying to sell to the group, and he doesn't let them in. This type of person can be a major turnoff to others in the group or those thinking about joining. No one wants to be in a Group where they're constantly going to be sold to.

At the end of the day, Sutton believes if you're interested in starting a group, whether on Facebook or somewhere else online or in your community, the key is to be genuine and to actually care about your group and its members. If you're only out to make cash, the community will see it and won't give you the attention you want. Plus, there are enough Joe Schmoe's out there who only want to sell you something. Don't be a Joe Schmoe.

Similar to Facebook, Twitter is a great way to reach more people and further establish yourself as an authority.

-------------- Roadmap --------------

1. Search for Groups on Facebook using the keywords you have decided on.
2. Join the Facebook Groups that you find.

3. Engage in the groups: like, comment, and help others.

4. Friend request the group admin and create a relationship with him or her.

5. Look through everyone who is engaged in each group, friend request them, and create a relationship.

6. Start your own Facebook Group. Create a title and design a cover photo, then invite your following. Use your twenty-five content post ideas and break them down into micro pieces of content of quotes and principles. Add to your content calendar.

7. Introduce all new members and friend request them and create a one-on-one relationship in the private messages.

8. Poll the group for engagement and to learn what topics they are interested in learning more about.

9. Find content tied to your industry or topic and share with the group.

Chapter 34

TWITTER HACKS

T witter, the social media giant that allows you to say what you want in 280 characters or less, really got adoption with two features: the @ mention allowing you to communicate directly with the brand or person associated with that handle, and the hashtag (#) allowing you to organize all of the mentions and conversations under that specific hashtag. What's great about both is that it's easy to find and search brands and personalities to learn what they're working on and communicate with them directly.

Not every handle associated with a username communicates regularly, or at all. This is a no-no. Social media is a two-way street. If someone is communicating or mentioning you, have a conversation back with them, help them, or do what they ask. If they ask a question, respond. There are several ways to communicate back, including a retweet, which takes their content and shares it on your feed.

If both parties follow each other, they can have direct message conversations which can only be seen by them. If someone likes your tweet, go ahead and react back to them and continue the conversation. A response is also limited to 280 characters. Posts can be text only, images, or video.

The Twitter feed is similar to a Facebook feed in that it allows you to see the content of those whom you follow. Unlike Facebook though, you see all posted content since Twitter doesn't have an algorithm that only shows you bits and pieces. This is great because you can follow the brands and personalities that you want and consume all of their content. When you see something you enjoy or want to respond to, send them a response. Using Twitter to your advantage can get you seen by others to help you with things like finding a job, building up credibility, and creating new relationships.

Twitter should be used to show off what you're best at by creating engaging and desired content, while using hashtags to help it be seen by those who already are using those same hashtags. Do this while creating new relationships with other industry experts and people looking to learn more from you. To stand out, be sure to maximize your profile with the tips from Chapter 24, as well as adding hashtags that speak to your skills, talents, offerings, etc. To determine what makes for a good hashtag, search Twitter and use your keywords with a (#) in front of them and see what you find. If there's a lot of recent content by thousands, it's likely a good hashtag to use. You can also use HashTagify as a tool to search top hashtags.

With all social media, there's no set strategy as to what works and what doesn't. If a platform has multiple features, try them all to see which receives the most engagement. With Twitter, this means trying different times of days, varying the length of your posts, possibly including images/videos, mentioning a handle, etc. If you continue to post and receive no retweets or likes and your following doesn't grow, this is an indication that you should try a new strategy. Just because you're not getting engagement doesn't mean your content sucks. It could mean that the people who want to see and engage with your content are not following you. So, you have to go out and find them.

Twitter Chats are a great way to educate, get new followers, and be seen as an expert in the hashtag or topic of a group. **A Twitter Chat is a forum-based conversation for a short period of time where a number of questions are asked to a panel who provides their answers and feedback.** A Twitter Chat is not limited exclusively to the forum guests or those who were promoted to be on the Twitter Chat, so you can jump in and provide your answers to the questions that the host asks.

Use this opportunity to introduce yourself to both the host and other panel members and get in front of the crowd who originally came for the host panel. By providing the best answers, you can easily get dozens to hundreds of new followers in one single Twitter Chat. Then, just like you would on Facebook, create a relationship with those new followers by reaching out. You can do this by asking to follow each other and then head to the direct messages (DMs) where you can have a one-on-one conversation. Or, if you prefer, you can stay in the public chat and converse there. Either works to create a relationship and once you have a stronger relationship, ask to set up a meeting with them on the phone or Skype or, if they live near you, arrange a time to meet up for coffee.

No matter who the person is, whether you think they're important or not, *always* create a relationship. You never know who *they* know and how they can help you, and more importantly, how you can help them. It can't be said enough how much people appreciate you helping them. Besides the fact that we need more helpful people in this world, the people you help almost always want to reciprocate and help you in return.

As discussed in the media chapter, Twitter is a great place to create relationships with brands that have big followings. The brands could be media, businesses, personalities, or handles with a lot of followers. These popular or influential handles have clout that, if you can get a sliver of approval from them, can give you clout as well and help to get you some attention from their followers.

Bob Burg is the author of several books, with his most popular, *The Go-Giver,* selling over 700,000 copies. A go-giver is someone who understands, has learned, or is always intuitively shifting their focus from getting to giving. In the business world, giving is the process of providing value to others. By doing so it's not only a pleasant way to do business, it's almost always a profitable way to do business.

Burg has a strong following on Twitter and has a true knack for getting engagement from his fans. He doesn't just broadcast to his followers, but he also engages back with a public response to every tweet, even if it's just a simple thank you. His technique is refreshing because even with his 100,000-plus Twitter following, Burg isn't cocky and doesn't give off the feeling that he is super famous. This best-selling author speaks in front of crowds of 16,000 and even charges $25,000 to speak to an organization. These numbers are mentioned because he still cares, and it shows in his work, in his social media, and in everything he does. Not only when he receives a tweet does he respond back, but when he receives a retweet he creates a new tweet thanking those who gave him love. These are super-easy ways to engage, instead of only broadcasting to your following. Even with a super brand like Burg's, he doesn't just preach the "give" mindset, he acts on it by constantly providing value to his targets and engaging with them.

Twitter is basically a modern-day newsfeed, yet unlike in years past, you get the content you want to receive and the ability for those whom you follow to engage back with you. Through the past decade a relatively unknown forum-based site, Reddit, has grown quite the following underground and is now one of the most heavily trafficked sites.

------------- Roadmap --------------

1. If you have not yet, join Twitter.
2. Upload a boring image of you or your brand, boring as in awesome!
3. Create and upload a cover photo the describes you.
4. Write and upload a description that includes your big wins, who you are, and relevant hashtags in your industry.
5. Search for Twitter Chats: "#keywordhashtags + #twitterchat."
6. Engage in conversations.
7. Follow the moderators, panelists, and those engaging. Create one-on-one relationships.
8. Add content for Twitter to your content calendar.

Chapter 35

PROVING YOURSELF ON REDDIT

Unlike Facebook and Twitter, Reddit (and Quora) do index their content which can be found at a direct link. This is a gold mine for content lovers. Again, Facebook and Twitter are great tools to build up your brand and following in the present, but if you posted something amazing two years ago, it's not easy to find. Both Reddit and Quora are forums that track, index, and allow you, the content provider or answerer, the ability to have repeatable searchable content. It would suck to do all this work, creating messaging and content, and go from being seen by many to seemingly disappearing off the face of the earth simply because an algorithm changes, especially when it's something you have no control over!

Reddit, one of the most popular websites in the world, is a great tool to learn about a topic you want to educate yourself or business on. Through a semi-anonymous screen name, it also gives you the ability to be highlighted by the answers you provide. Reddit's organized into a series of communities called "Subreddits." Each Subreddit is led by a group of moderators who you could identify as the top experts under that Subreddit or category. This doesn't mean they're the top expert in the world, but they have to be fairly knowledgeable in order to start or take over a Subreddit.

Reddit also has a main page that propagates the top posts for everyone to see. To begin, search your keywords and see if there are Subreddits for your search. Create a free account and begin to see what people are commenting on and then create posts around those topics. Reddit doesn't encourage a user to blatantly promote their business. Rather, they have an upvote/downvote system for users to try to police content the overall group does or doesn't agree with or like.

Sometimes it's tough to tell whether or not you're self-promoting. For example, if your business can directly solve the problem someone is writing about, you can probably preface your answer with a disclaimer explaining that your business may be able to help. Or maybe you wrote a blog post about the exact thing someone is discussing in Reddit. You want to post the link saying, "Hey, I wrote this a few weeks ago, I think it may help." Depending on the Subreddit, that may or may not be violating their rules so make sure you know the rules. You don't want to get kicked out of a community that you may be able to benefit from in the future. Make sure you read all of the rules before posting. Each community is different and moderated by different people.

Find a Subreddit that is appropriate for you. For example, if you're looking to learn more about small business, you would search small business and find several Subreddits focused on different aspects of business. With hundreds of new posts every day, these Subreddits are a great place for you to learn from others, engage with them, get your name out, and help them in return. There's no best time to post or engage, so simply engage when it works best for your schedule.

Once you're signed up for Reddit, find posts you can help with and provide a response. Reddit uses a points system called Karma. Always keep in mind that the more you help others and engage with other posts, the higher your Karma score. Think of your Karma score as an indicator of how your responses are scored or valued. If you have a few points, engage more. When you receive upvotes on your posts or responses, your Karma score also increases.

Provide feedback on twenty-five posts and then ask a question of your own. You can even add this to your calendar on your phone to receive notifications. If you're questioning what blog content or video to shoot, go to Reddit and see what forum posts are getting the most engagement. You can see engagement by the responses and by the post score. On the most popular, and relevant to you, posts, use the answers to create compelling blog posts with keyword-heavy content with several external links and expert answers to improve the quality of your content.

Once the blog post is finished, you can add a quick response and, if allowed, post the link to the popular Reddit post. Or you can link the Reddit post in the blog post so others can follow along. You can also direct message the users in the Subreddit who engaged the most and ask for their feedback.

Don't just message them and say, "Hey, I wrote this. Now read it." Ask for feedback, as most will provide more thoughts on the topic. And bonus, you have now made a new friend. By asking for feedback, you're showing that you respect the user that you reached out to and that makes them feel special and valued.

Many Subreddits have a sidebar set of links you can use to learn more about the topic of the Subreddit. You can also create a relationship with the moderators and become active in the group. Once that relationship is strong, ask the moderator if they can add you as a moderator and a link to your content on the side bar. It may also make sense to create your own Subreddit along with becoming a moderator of one that you have strong ties to. By creating your own Subreddit, you would have to do all of the legwork to make it popular, but if you can work it up to receiving a lot of engagement, you can leverage all the relationships in the Subreddit to become the anomaly.

-------------- **Roadmap** --------------

1. Sign up for Reddit. Remember your username can be anonymous.
2. Search for relevant Subreddits and engage with posts that resonate with you through an up- or downvote. Comment when you have extra to provide. Do not just post a link about you as you will likely get flagged and removed.
3. After you have engaged on twenty-five posts, create your own question in the Subreddit that you frequent the most. (Do not just upvote the first twenty-five posts, that is cheating.)
4. Look into becoming a moderator on a favorite Subreddit or create your own. If you join an existing Subreddit, create a relationship with the current moderator(s).

Chapter 36

USING QUORA TO
BECOME AN AUTHORITY

Quora is a forum similar to Reddit but is more user-friendly. It's a question and answer forum broken into topics, whereas Reddit's topics and anything related to the topic go under that specific Subreddit. It has much of the functionality that other forums have, however, you're not anonymous to semi-anonymous. You have a profile page that allows you to briefly describe who you are, along with providing links to some of your work. All of the questions and answers that you provide are publicly viewed—nothing is hidden. Quora refers to expertise as "Knows About." Your profile is also lined with a credentials portion to give a snapshot of who you are and your total Quora viewership. Obviously, the more eyeballs you have, the more credible a source you are to the Quora crowd.

Start by signing up for a free Quora account and filling out the required information. If you created a document to house all of your social media profile information as suggested in Chapter 24, this should be a fairly simple copy and paste. Once you're set up, begin in a similar fashion to Reddit by providing help and answers to those who are asking questions.

As you peruse the site, you'll see questions you may feel comfortable with and confident in answering. To get bigger impact, try to comment on posts that have several answers already. Although it may be a repeat of a previous answer, provide it in your own voice. It's possible that your answer is easier for others to comprehend or is more engaging. This gets eyeballs on your comment.

Start by answering twenty-five questions people have posted. You can receive notifications on topics you preselect via email, or simply go to the categories you think you can provide feedback for and start replying. Just like the first step of a sales funnel, or trying to become an authority, it's not about selling why you're the best, it's instead an opportunity for you to get in front of new prospects and provide them value by getting them answers to their questions. And even better, since Quora indexes this content, it lives forever and is searchable to a user on Quora and through a search engine. That networking event where you answered questions for three people becomes digital networking where you can now potentially reach millions.

Once your viewership has grown, think about asking a few questions of your own on topics that *you* want to learn more about. Users want to see that you don't just provide feedback, but that you want to engage and have a thirst for learning. If you're wondering where to find content to comment on, search for one of your keywords. Let's say it's on marketing. Quora starts with the best answers, which typically number in the hundreds. Not every Quora posts gets a lot of eyeballs, so if you want to be seen start with posts that have a lot of answers and feedback already since these are the most popular. Go down the list Quora provides, like you would a Google search. Click on the topics most relevant to you until you find the one that's best. It's possible to comment on every single post. Again, provide your feedback even if it's similar to someone else's because your copy could be more receptive or easier to understand than someone else's. It's also just a good idea to comment on popular posts as they give you the best chance to get more users looking at your comments and ultimately you.

Be sure to add time in your schedule to regularly go into Quora and provide feedback. Use calendar reminders if necessary. If you're looking for content ideas, look for inspiration from the questions others are asking. You can take these questions and use them on the groups you manage or even create content around others' answers for your social media posts. If you see one answer getting a lot of feedback, create an image quoting the response and post it on social media with a tag and source to the person who provided it. By doing so, you're promoting them and creating a new relationship. Everyone loves to be given credit. It proves that they know what they're talking about.

If you were an author for the *Oxford Journal,* you would want others to give you a hat tip and say that your words were meaningful, powerful, and provide a ridiculous amount of value. Just like you were creating relationships with influencers in the past chapters, if you can take messaging that they already said and promote it for them, you're leveraging their clout and helping them get seen by more people. The "give before you get" mindset is one that can be hard for someone to comprehend, but in the digital world where everyone is doing the same thing, or the cable salesman is annoying everyone with the same cold call every day, you need a strategy to catch the eye of others. Marketing is simply getting someone's attention first. If you can't get someone to look up from playing a game or their Snapchat feed, all of the remaining pieces of a campaign are worthless.

Help others and ensure you have a maximized profile and you'll begin to see results. You'll find that others begin looking at you as an authority in your subject or field. To become the anomaly, you must find ways to project how you're different and know what you're talking about. Provide value, give before you get, and before you know it, people will be begging you for more.

Constantly getting in front of hundreds of people online helps grow your brand. But how can you get in front of hundreds of people in person? Another great way to be an expert and authority is through landing speaking gigs. There are hundreds of events happening in every community every month and chances are they're looking for a speaker like you.

-------------- **Roadmap** --------------

1. Sign up for Quora.
2. Maximize your profile.
3. Search and follow categories that are relevant to you/your brand and the keywords/key phrases you have selected.

4. Engage with posts in which you have answers to provide.
5. Share your engagements on Twitter and Facebook.
6. Ask a question.

Chapter 37

LANDING SPEAKING GIGS

Speaking gigs introduce you to a group of prospects who may have never heard of you. In the past chapters, we have focused on primarily online solutions, however, speaking to a crowd who is interested in your topics can be a wonderful introduction to you and your brand. It can also be a highly lucrative one as many can pay good money for a short period of time on stage. **Speaking gigs are typically a scheduled affair in which you provide your expertise to a qualified crowd.** It's similar to your blog or webinar content but in front of a live audience. If the audience loves you and your message, there's great potential to move them through the sales funnel.

If you're not one who likes to get in front of people, start small with opportunities in your local community at clubs such as Rotary, Kiwanis, or Toastmasters. These of course are not paid speaking gigs, nor do they get you in front of your target audience, but they do allow you to get an understanding of what it's like to speak on your topic in front of strangers. You should seek opportunities as often as possible to practice and to keep from stumbling over your words. Just remember, your audience is not expecting you to be a fantastic public speaker. They do, however, expect you to be knowledgeable about your subject.

If you create a PowerPoint presentation, don't just read from the slides. You also don't want to have so many words on the slides that all your audience is doing is reading the slides instead of listening to you. Instead, use your slides as a complementary feature to enhance your presentation. You should be able to give your presentation without needing the slides at all to keep the audience focused on you. To get your audience to stay engaged throughout your presentation, ask questions that the audience can respond to by raising their hands, standing up, or other movements that get them to loosen up and stay focused on you. Nobody wants someone to doze off, so keep them engaged and awake!

As you're showing the world that you're an anomaly, make sure to post a copy of your talks (and any associated slides) online.

Meetups and conferences help you get your message across and are filled with target customers and other industry experts who, if they like what they hear, start following you and, hopefully, telling people in their networks about you. To find the correct meetups and conferences, use the appropriate keywords to search the Meetup site and/or the city (or cities) where you want to speak. Once you find a Meetup or conference where you want to speak, reach out to the organizer to learn the process of becoming a presenter at their next event.

For a small meetup (less than 50 people), it should be fairly simple to get connected with the organizer and speak at the next event. For a larger convention or conference, many of them have a call for speakers where they ask for a more detailed explanation of the speaker's topic. A group of organizers then gets together and selects a speaker based on those descriptions. Some of the questions they might ask range from wanting to know the title of your talk and who your target audience is and their experience level, to the length of your talk and what outcomes or takeaways the audience can expect. It's smart to create an ongoing file of all of this copy so it's an easy copy and paste if you begin to apply to speak at a lot of conferences.

If you're a startup looking for a group to practice your pitch, 1 Million Cups is a weekly business-friendly meetup in 100-plus cities across the U.S. They have up to two businesses a week pitch their business to the group. This is great way to practice, learn what others think of your venture, get feedback on your business, and network with others who could become customers, teammates, mentors, investors, and/or supporters. This is a free group to join and they're always accepting submission requests from businesses wanting to present.

When giving a talk, follow the Problem, Solution, and Traction Method, which is as simple as it seems. If you don't answer something for someone, they can always ask during the Q&A time.

Gary Plaag is an experienced public speaker with over 500 performances in his storied career. Even with decades of experience under his belt, he knows that if he wants to continue to grow his network, he has to get out and provide more value to his prospects and targets. He does this primarily through speaking engagements to teach the audience how to improve their speaking skills. Fear of public speaking is most people's top fear, so if Plaag can get in front of his targets and help them overcome or at least ease their fear, he is providing great value to them. Then he sets up a one-on-one meeting with them. If during the one-on-one he finds that they fit the bill, he brings them through each step of the funnel.

To land a speaking gig, Plaag believes you must know who your customer is. To find these groups, leverage networking and let the organizers know you're interested in speaking to their audience. When looking for your target audience, think about how to diversify your client base so that you have more opportunities to speak. Look for patterns in who your most common customers are and create consumer profiles based on those. If you own a coffee shop, these profiles might be freelancers, writers, stay-at-home moms, professors, and retired folks. These are all very different customers and can be found at different types of events.

When speaking, it's a good idea to use your cellphone or other device to record the talk. This is helpful for two reasons: You can review and critique your talk and you can post the content online to create podcasts and blog posts from it. If you can afford to, hire a videographer to record your speech. If you can't afford a professional, invest in recording equipment. Since audio is the most important, if you can only afford one piece of equipment, make sure it's high-quality audio equipment. This does not mean break the bank to buy a really expensive microphone. If you can't buy, you can always rent. Many libraries and some universities provide equipment rentals. If you know you're about to do a talk, reach out to your local university system and create a relationship with the communication or media departments to see if you can get an intern to create content for you in exchange for course credit, or for a class project. Find film students looking for opportunities to use the skills they're learning. You could end up with a high-quality product, so reach out and ask for help.

Practicing your presentation at local events helps you home in on some of your weaknesses when it comes to public speaking. When speaking, understand that *everyone* gets nervous, even those who do public speaking on a regular basis. It's completely natural to get nervous. All your audience wants is to learn from you. And if you don't think you're necessarily a great speaker, don't force yourself to try to become one. Instead, focus on making your performances stronger as described above. The biggest thing is to provide as much value to your audience as you can. That's what you're there for, and that's what they want.

Instead of memorizing a speech word for word, have a good understanding of your material and outline, and speak in your natural voice. If you memorize, you take the risk of missing a line, messing up, and not knowing what to do next because you're out of order. If you do mess up a line or fumble, don't sweat it, and *don't* tell your audience that you have made a mistake. Instead, roll with the punches and continue. Don't show defeat.

Before you speak, attend or watch as many other speeches as you can, and observe what works and what doesn't. Find what you like from other presenters and learn how you can adopt these methods. You can attend community events, conferences, or watch videos online. Try not to watch edited videos, but instead find those in "raw" form. These provide more insight than an edited version.

If you're performing at an event that allows time for Q&A, always welcome feedback, even if you don't agree with it. Whatever you do, *don't* become confrontational on the stage. Accept the feedback and take a mental note. Be thankful that you have engagement! Also, understand who is providing the feedback or asking the questions. Oftentimes those who ask questions could become customers, so be certain to create a relationship with them after.

If you're having trouble finding a good first place to land a speaking gig, you can always create your own event. Hosting events and meetups can do several things for your brand. A meetup or conference makes you appear as more of an authority. Target customers will come to you to learn and network, and then you teach them, and they become part of your "tribe." In the next chapter, you'll learn how to host a meetup, what topics your attendees are looking for, how to find attendees and invite them, and how to turn a meetup into deal flow.

-------------- **Roadmap** --------------

1. Search and add speaking places/gigs to your AMR document. Search your keywords + your city + speaking opportunities in a search engine or on Meetup and Eventbrite.
2. Create a relationship with organizers and offer your presentation to their group.
3. Practice your performance beforehand.
4. Record performance and review.

Chapter 38

ORGANIZING AND HOSTING MEETUPS

To be seen and stand out amongst a crowd, consider hosting a meetup. **A meetup is typically an educational meeting with a group of your target customers around a topic they want to learn about.** Instead of writing a blog or hosting a podcast, you're getting your content out face-to-face. It doesn't scale like the other methods, but it can be a great avenue to build trust in your community.

Meetups, conferences, workshops, and events take time to plan and execute, but are a tremendously valuable tool in shaping you and your brand to become a top dog in your field. To get started, understand what will be the content you base your event around. Just as if you were writing a blog post, you want to think about your target customer and their needs, and what they're looking for. When you name your event, be sure to be keyword rich so when people search for your event or content, your event comes up in the search.

Your content or topic is the single most important reason someone will attend your meetup. If the content is not what your target customer is looking for, they will not attend. When you're channel surfing on your television, what makes you stop and watch? Something that intrigues you or material that piques your curiosity. Your meetup topics have to have the same effect on your target audience.

Can you create a series of meetups around a topic? If you're an artist, you could teach newbies how to get started in art or how to set up a canvas. You're an expert in your field even if you don't believe it. You understand your craft better than most and people want to learn how to do what you do. A dummies guide to a topic is also a good option for a series. If you're a marketing firm, you can bring in prospects and share best practices on search engine optimization or branding.

Try hosting a guest speaker forum with industry experts in your field. This way you have multiple speakers promoting your event with your name all over it. To be the anomaly, you want to be seen everywhere. Leveraging an existing brand to promote yours allows you to have an unbelievable multiplier effect.

You can also host a recap of a project you have recently wrapped up. If you share how you put together your product(s), people who attend will take pictures, and share with their networks, which gets you more exposure.

Invite guests into your office. By hosting at your office, you bring prospects to you and help them solve their problems in a hands-on fashion. Perhaps you're a technology firm that builds iPhone applications for your customers. You could host a meetup and share how businesses can use apps to build their business. A lot of businesses want an app but have no idea how to go about getting one built, the costs associated, or what the benefits are in helping to grow their brand. By hosting a meetup that delivers those answers, not only do you have a prime audience, but you have also provided them significant value.

If you work from home or remotely, or simply don't have an office, you have many options available to host you including libraries, co-working spaces, incubators, recreation centers, restaurants, and even borrowing a friend's office (preferably with their permission). As your event grows, you may need to pay for a venue, but when starting out, don't spend a lot of (if any) money for a space.

Once you have a name and a location, and have chosen a date, you'll need to put those details on a website or event page such as Meetup or Eventbrite. These tools have great reminder systems in place, so you don't have to keep up with your guests and their RSVPs.

Add an event description with details on what the event is, who the event is for, when the event is happening, where the event is held, and what the major takeaways are. As you complete events, get testimonials and results from your audience. You can add those to the description if you do the same event in the future.

Don't forget to remind your guests 48 hours before the event to see if they still plan to attend and if there are any questions about the event.

On the day of the meetup, have a signup sheet to get more detailed contact information, what they hope to learn more about, or what their pain points are. People will provide you way more detailed answers than you think. You'll then have a list of ideas for upcoming meetups, plus new contacts with which to connect and dive deeper.

For the meetup, post an itinerary with set expectations, and then follow them. There's nothing worse than saying one thing and letting another happen. You lose credibility and your audience gets mad. Introduce yourself and tell people why they're there and then get into your content for the meetup. Be sure to have time built in at the end for Q&A and networking. People love to meet other people. After the event has wrapped up, thank everyone for attending and let them know about any future events. Also, ask them to share with their networks how the event went and that they should attend the next one.

Within 24 hours, send a follow-up message thanking your audience and recap the evening. Anything you said you would send them, do so at this time. You may have mentioned documents or additional resources associated with your talk. Don't fail to deliver on this!

If you believe your event went well and can turn into customers, rinse and repeat early and often. Throw as many events as you can successfully manage. Events are a great way to get your customers in the door but few take advantage of these opportunities.

Events put me on the map. Back in 2010, meetups were unknown in my southeastern Virginia town. I was still a nobody, fresh out of my TV news career. I didn't have a network of business friends or any relationships with business owners. But, I did have an office where we helped businesses build their software. To get exposure for these businesses, we would host social media and business owner meetups where attendees could share best practices and how-tos. What started as a dozen people grew into an email list in the thousands of prospects itching to learn but unable to find anyone willing to teach them. Meetups were an opportunity that were staring me in the face.

Almost a decade later, this network that was built through the events I hosted has provided many amazing opportunities for me. With over 1,000 events in the bag as of today, I am seen as an authority in business and marketing. The topics I speak about and educate people on are focused around those ideas of helping people grow through what they're best at. Giving them an avenue to understand how they can share it with their followers allows them to gain more exposure, credibility, and customers. If you're on the fence about events, let my story encourage you to start hosting some. Yes, they can be time-consuming, but the results they've provided me and my business are more than worth it.

Before Zvi Band founded the popular CRM and contact management platform Contactually, he started DC Tech Meetup. Band realized through networking that he had made a lot of connections but those connections didn't know each other. Knowing that there was a burgeoning startup scene in the nation's capital, he wanted to pair that scene with other networks who were unaware that the tech movement was coming out of its shell. He set out to make Proudly Made in DC, a directory of businesses located in the Washington, D.C., area. This business gained attention, quickly making its way to the *New York Times* website. Many cities across the world have now replicated their own version of Proudly Made. DC Tech Meetup brought together many of the companies on Proudly Made and others interested in the startup scene. The first meetup had 150 attendees. Now each meetup has just under 1,000 attendees and is one of the most popular and recognized active meetups in the world.

Each meetup showcases a handful of new startups based in D.C., but ultimately Band wants everyone in the room to meet each other, so they leave ample time for the networking and connections to occur. Band believes these connections have helped not only the D.C. market become known as one where startups are thriving, but also helped his personal brand and Contactually get in front of more prospects.

Being able to connect and resonate with your audience is crucial. When you're face-to-face with someone, it's much easier to establish a solid connection. You can see their emotions and mannerisms, and really connect with them. But how can you resonate with someone online? It's difficult to stand out online since there are millions of other people, but there are little things you can do here and there to help get someone's attention. One of my favorite vehicles for this is email marketing. Often overlooked, email can be extremely powerful when used correctly. Email marketing can be a huge moneymaker for your brand. It's one of the most used platform for brands to connect directly with their audiences.

-------------- **Roadmap** --------------

1. Decide what type of meetup you want to host.
2. Determine who should attend, why should they attend, title of meetup, time and location, what they'll receive, what takeaways they'll have, and who else they should expect to meet in attendance.
3. Take answers from #2 and create a landing page event on your website, on Eventbrite, or on Meetup. Collect guests' contact information.
4. Invite guests.
5. Set up and send emails to send 48 hours before the event and 24 hours after the event that include important information about the event.

Chapter 39

EMAIL MARKETING

E mail marketing is a clever way to get someone's attention. But, if your email never gets opened, it makes things a little difficult. In this chapter, you'll learn how to create an email marketing campaign, what to put in the email, and clever tricks to boost your open rate.

It's important to first understand what email marketing is. **When you email someone from your email platform, you're emailing that individual one-on-one, but when you have fans who subscribe to receive more information from you, it's email marketing.** You can email from your email platform, but you have to individually send each message every time, whereas marketing automation platforms allow you to create campaigns in advance and send multiple emails on a frequency and schedule you set. You can also track open rates, click rates, purchasing, etc. You can also try A/B testing, which is sending two similar emails with slight differences to see what works best. You can test things like which button color gets the most clicks, which subject line gets the most opens, which headline gets the most clicks, etc.

You may have wanted to do email marketing in the past but were too afraid of the time or technology behind it. Both have become simple, even for a not-so-tech-savvy person.

One change that has caused concern for email marketing campaigns is the promotions tab on clients like Gmail. Instead of going to your direct inbox, emails get sent to a folder or catch-all tab designated for spam or sales emails. Not everyone looks at these folders, so you can have great content, but it'll go unseen. It's encouraged to get your recipients to "double opt-in," which means to subscribe to a list and then confirm through email. This ensures the emails arrive in a main folder rather than a promotions tab (if you send an email using your standard email platform, it doesn't go to the promotions folders).

Before you start a campaign, you need to get set up with an email provider like Gmail, Yahoo, Hotmail, or Outlook. Once you have an email client, you can sign up for a marketing automation platform like Mailchimp, ActiveCampaign, or ConvertKit. Starting costs less than the price of this book. However, once you start growing the size of your email list, costs increase.

Let's focus on how to grow your first 100 subscribers. **A subscriber is someone looking for you to provide them additional information, content, laughs, or whatever content you provide.** It's basically someone giving you approval that they want more. Score! Think of this as Step 2 in the sales funnel.

Setting up campaigns is fairly easy and should be a series of content that you send on a predetermined schedule. This is often referred to as a drip campaign. If it's Tuesday at 9 p.m. when you send your first email, consider sending your weekly emails at that same time. It's a marketing tool to remind people when they can expect more from you. But don't lie; if you aren't going to send a weekly email, don't say you will.

To get your first 100 subscribers, go through your existing network and invite those who will find your content relevant. Tell them that you would love for them to subscribe. Not everyone will subscribe; I'm sure you have 100 or more people in your network that would find your content relevant to them. You can also ask them to share it with their networks, and preferably directly with someone who they think might find it helpful. Try to understand to the best of your ability what

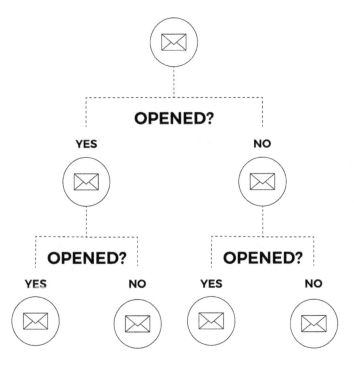

they're subscribing for. The more detailed you can be the better. Think about who your target customer is and what they're looking for, and then deliver it to them in these campaigns.

If your business is to help other businesses get started, your campaign could be a series of emails that include tips on how to start a business. If you're a comedian, it could be highlights of your best shows. Typically, these emails are *not* just sales emails to buy what you're selling. You have to educate and become the authority and get the respect of your subscribers before you start selling. You can sell, just not in every email. Remember when every day you would get an email from Groupon selling you something? Those days are over and don't work anymore. People want quality information that can help them, not a Girl Scout constantly trying to get you to buy cookies.

To get ongoing subscribers, create options throughout your existing content. You can do this in your email signature, social media profiles, blog posts, or even on an event check-in sheet. Make it a quick one-line message of what you provide to your viewers in return for their contact information.

- "Get free access to our weekly business tips on how to grow your real estate empire."
- "A seven-day course teaching you how to master Photoshop"
- "A monthly calendar of CrossFit events in your city"

There's always someone looking for answers. Answers that are cheaper, quicker, smarter, and easier. Be that solution and provide it through your email campaigns.

Remember that just because you do an action doesn't mean you'll get a reaction. Email subject lines are one of the most critical parts of an email. Think of it like a newspaper or Twitter feed. You stop when you see a headline or something that catches your attention. To get someone's attention, think about writing subject lines that are quick, or exactly what the email is going to be about. An email subject line should be written as if it were a text message. With so many people on the move and consuming an overwhelming majority of their content on smartphones, using this method will help you get people to open your emails.

Subject lines could be:

- "Hey"
- "Introduction"
- "Meeting Request on Date"
- "Weekly Calendar of Events"
- Or one that's a bit different using emojis

One technique that also works well is including someone's name: "Hey, Zack" or "Meeting Request with Zack."

Get creative and test what works and what doesn't. Email marketing is huge. It's an avenue for you to get direct access to your customers inbox, which unlike social media is a gem. Continue to create value and provide your subscribers what you promised. Two things that most people can create to share with their lists and followers are maps and calendars.

-------------- **Roadmap** --------------

1. Sign up for a free marketing automation platform like MailChimp, or for a small fee sign up for Active Campaign or ConvertKit.
2. Create and name your first email list (the group of contact information of people looking to engage with your content).
3. What kind of content will your subscribers receive and at what frequency?
4. Create a form for your following to sign up for your list (add simple contact information: email, name, and maybe address).
5. Add "Sign up for our email list" to your content calendar.
6. Get your first 100 subscribers.

Chapter 40

BUILDING CALENDARS AND MAPS

Populating a calendar with events in your market or industry can be an easy way to be an anomaly and get a ton of followers. In the fitness world, there are many different races, triathlons, and bodybuilding events, but is there a go-to place where you can compile a list—curated or in total—that breaks down, markets, and showcases these events? Events are everywhere, and while Meetup and Eventbrite share events, they don't house every event in a market. Many are under the radar and use their own internal system to market instead of a third-party tool. If you create a calendar of events showcasing all of the events in your industry, you can become a source to not only the event host, but also their customers who are looking for events to attend, too.

Start by deciding if you're going to include every event in your niche or if you're going to curate and pick events you think are the best with some sort of commentary included as to why it made your list. You can brand the list to help with your branding needs and start perusing different events around your market or industry. You can do this for the city you want exposure in or, if you're a worldwide brand, think about doing one for the world. Now, if you do worldwide, you likely will do curated because it'll be impossible to find every event globally.

By creating an inclusive calendar, visitors will come to you since you're providing them value in having multiple events in one place, plus you're saving them time since they don't have to go from site to site trying to find events.

Along with a calendar, there may be additional opportunities for you to populate a series of points on a map or directions to a specific location. Where2Wheel, an online community connecting Jeep owners with places to go off road, created a concept that allows Jeep owners to find trails. If you own a Honda Civic, you likely don't care, but Jeep owners are frequently looking for locations to go, as they call it, "muddin'." When the married co-founders Brittany and David Peregoff founded the company, they knew there was a community on the western side of the United States, but it was lacking on the East Coast. So, they set out to create a map with points of where a Jeep could legally go off road in that area of the country.

They found users by creating engaging Facebook campaigns that were quirky, like Jeeps that were upside down or driving through rivers. Things that a non-Jeep owner may think is ridiculous, but when you know your targets like the Peregoff's do, they understand that Jeep owners would flock to this content. And with 45,000-plus Facebook fans, they receive engagement from over 95 percent of their following. They follow a three-step concept—research similar pages and see what's popular, get an emotional response as that gets a ton of engagement, and they share information from other companies in the industry which helps get attention from other brands.

-------------- **Roadmap** --------------

1. First, determine if you have an opportunity to curate a set of calendars/events/maps. If yes, what will you curate and why should someone care (e.g., saving time)?
2. Pull all pertinent and relevant data points and combine on calendar or map.
3. Share your calendar or map with your following.
4. Add content to your content calendar and distribute.

Chapter 41

THE END

My high school graduation is a blur. Not because I was drunk. Rather, because it was so long ago. One thing about it does stick out in my head, though. The guest speaker rambled for who knows how long. And at the end he said, "You won't remember this talk, but you'll remember Fig Newtons, so remember that."

All these years later, that is all I remember.

So, running out like the Ultimate Warrior would to his WrestleMania entrance, this book has come to an end.

Why? Because if you remember anything from this book, it's that it just ended unlike any other book. Remember, Fig Newtons. If we correspond and you say you read the book and I ask you for the password, this is it. If you want to stand out, you have to be different—you have to be…the Anomaly.

The End.

ABOUT THE AUTHOR

 Zack Miller started his first business at the age of 10. Since then he's spent decades helping other people successfully start, grow, and dominate their businesses through his company, Hatch. Zack has used the skills detailed in his book *Anomaly* to land an interview with Daymond John, host a business TV show on ABC, talk business at the White House, get featured in *Entrepreneur* magazine, and raise money from the team that started The Weather Channel. Check out Zack on his podcast, *Zack Miller Says*. He currently resides in Norfolk, VA.